Illuminate
Publishing

WJEC
GCSE

Film Studies

Study and Revision Guide

Jackie Newman
Dave Fairclough
Jackie Dearden

Published in 2014 by Illuminate Publishing Ltd, P.O. Box 1160,
Cheltenham, Gloucestershire GL50 9RW

Orders: Please visit www.illuminatepublishing.com
or email sales@illuminatepublishing.com

British Library Cataloguing in Publication Data

A catalogue record for this book is available from the British Library

ISBN 978-1-908682-20-8

Printed by CPI Group (UK) Ltd, Croydon, CR0 4YY

06.16

The publisher's policy is to use papers that are natural, renewable and recyclable products
made from wood grown in sustainable forests. The logging and manufacturing processes
are expected to conform to the environmental regulations of the country of origin.

Copyright note:

This material has been endorsed by WJEC and offers high quality support for the delivery
of WJEC qualifications. While this material has been through a WJEC quality assurance
process, all responsibility for the content remains with the publisher.

Editor: Geoff Tuttle

Design and layout: Nigel Harriss

Cover photograph: Warner Bros / The Kobal Collection

Acknowledgements

The authors and publisher wish to thank the following for their contributions to this book:
Leo Dearden, Jack Sutcliffe, James and Tom Clegg

Dedication

JN – Thanks to Julie and Triestina, two inspirational teachers, and Cleggie my 'rock'.
DF – I would like to thank all my mums and dads – you know who you are.
JD – For Leo, the original guinea pig.

Contents

How to use this book

The contents of this study and revision guide are designed to help you succeed in your GCSE Film Studies examination. It has been written especially for the WJEC Film Studies course you are taking and includes helpful information, tips and ideas which will help you to perform well in the two examined papers and the Controlled Assessment tasks.

Knowledge and Understanding

Throughout the guide you will be given support to help you develop your responses to every area of the course. There are:

- Definitions of key terms and examples of the ways in which these can be used in order to help with your revision.
- Quickfire questions designed to test your knowledge and understanding.
- Quickfire answers to check at the end of each section. These should be combined with your own responses to create a useful bank of revision information for you to use.
- Tips designed to help you improve your examination technique and to support your creative work for the controlled tasks.

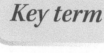

Key term

Exam tip

Section 2

Section 2 of the guide focuses upon Film Language. This aims to provide you with a strong foundation for studying, analysing and creating film. Your understanding of what constitutes film language, and your ability to consider and discuss how it communicates to an audience, is the key to success in all three elements of the examination.

The section on film language is broken up into two major parts:

- The 'micro' elements: mise-en-scène, cinematography, editing and sound.
- The 'macro' elements: genre, narrative, representation and ideologies.

Each of the 'micro' and 'macro' elements are initially considered separately in this section and each subsection begins with a 'tool kit for analysis'. This 'tool kit' contains specific film language vocabulary or key points that you should know and use when analysing film. Although the film language section separates each element, it is like any other language. So it is really important to consider how these elements work together to create meaning and response. The ways in which they combine form an integral part of what is covered in each of the five sections of this guide.

Terminology tool kit

Section 3

3: What is a Superhero?

Section 3

Section 3 of the guide covers Paper 1: Exploring Film. This is the paper that focuses on one film genre – in this case the Superhero genre. The questions asked in this examination are designed to assess your knowledge and understanding of the three key inter-related study areas which underpin the specification: film language, film industry and film audiences. This section takes you through Hollywood as probably the most important/influential example of film industry. It then examines what is meant by the term genre and how it is identified (its codes and conventions). It also looks at marketing, aiming to build upon your knowledge and understanding of the importance of genre to industry and audiences.

Section 4

Section 4 covers Paper 2: Exploring Film Outside Hollywood. This paper asks you to study one film produced outside Hollywood from a list of ten. The section firstly looks at industry issues, comparing the Hollywood product with films made elsewhere in the world. It then looks at three of the films on the list and takes you through:

● The representation of people, places, event and issues.

● How film language contributes to the representations.

Although the three films chosen may not be the ones you have studied, the key terms, the use of film language and ways of interrogating and expressing ideas about the representation of people, places, events and issues, are techniques that can be easily transferred to the study of your focus film.

Section 4 *Tsotsi*
3: Places – setting, themes and issues

Section 5

Section 5 focuses on Controlled Assessment, the internally assessed unit. This is your chance to demonstrate your ability to use creative and technical skills to research, analyse and construct film products. The section considers approaches to researching a film of your choice and then analysing two of the 'micro' elements of film language in a short sequence from that film. It also suggests appropriate formats together with technical tips for your pre-production and production choices. It will look at exemplar work from previous students outlining strengths and weaknesses. You will also be offered advice on producing an effective evaluative analysis of your production pieces.

Moderator feedback

Exam Practice and Technique

At the end of Sections 3 and 4 there is an opportunity to think about and practise your exam skills and techniques. You are given advice on taking notes, choosing and planning your answers. You will also look at the ways in which you can move from shorter to longer, more detailed answers, building your response step-by-step. There are some extracts from sample answers to possible kinds of questions that could appear in both examinations. The commentary on these will talk about the strengths and weaknesses of the answers. You will have an opportunity to make suggestions on possible improvements and to consider how you plan and develop ideas when moving from shorter to longer answers.

Section 3
12: Exam skills

Revision is the key to getting the grades you are capable of. It is your responsibility to make sure that you know what we mean when we talk about film language, film industry, or film audiences. You also need to be able to talk about these three key areas using the appropriate terminology. Finally, don't forget that we are all individuals and that we all respond to films in different ways. In terms of personal response there are no right or wrong answers. So identify, describe, analyse then respond in your own inimitable way and you will already be a long way on the road to exam success!

Section 1: Exploring Film

1: Studying film

Why study film?

Film is probably one of the most popular art forms in the world today. It is a major industry in most developed countries and an important part of people's cultural experience. All over the world films are being produced, sold and watched. They entertain us, educate and provoke debate. They appeal to our senses, can make us laugh or cry, and evoke a whole range of emotions in between. Most of us love to watch and talk about film; sometimes the themes and issues they deal with are familiar ones which affect us in our everyday lives. Sometimes they present the world in very simple terms and it is easy for us to identify hero from villain and right from wrong. This is a world where stories have happy endings, where right triumphs and we all leave the cinema 'feeling good'. Other times we are presented with a world where more complex moral and social questions are examined. Here there are few absolutes, characters do not have easy choices, and difficult moral questions are presented with no neat, or easy, solutions given. There may not be a happy ending and we may leave the cinema angry or upset but nevertheless still thinking it was a truly brilliant film.

How do we study film?

This WJEC Film Studies specification is designed to build upon your own experience of film as a consumer and a creator. It aims to encourage you to recognise and explore just how complicated this experience is in an increasingly **globalised**, interconnected environment. If you have opted for this course there is an assumption that you are keen to develop your enjoyment and understanding of the various aspects of film study. This involves developing a critical, investigative approach to learning about films, the film industry and film audiences. Developing this approach requires hard work and a real engagement with the subject, but it is work that can be very rewarding and enjoyable; work that opens up a whole new world of people, places, ideas, issues and events.

Key term

Globalised
Worldwide, universal, wide-ranging.

What do we study and why?

Starting with mainstream films this course allows you to study films and the ways they are experienced, the importance of visual representations in today's global society and the place film has in communicating ideas, attitudes and cultural beliefs, both today and in the past. You will approach the course through three study areas:

- The language of film – the elements that create meaning in films and the ways they are organised in order to tell a story to their audience.

- Film organisations – the film companies which make films. What is involved in the making of films and the ways in which they are sold and screened.

- Film audiences – how you respond to the films you watch, how other audiences respond and the issues raised across a range of films made for or about other people and places.

These areas are interconnected, they work together to give you a strong framework for studying and creating film.

Mr Wenger excites his students
Die Welle (The Wave) 2008

Finally, this course can provide a strong foundation should you want to continue learning about film when you go into Higher Education. In terms of future studies it is interesting to note that the film industry offers a huge amount of career opportunities. The chances of you becoming another Danny Boyle may be slim but just think of the range of exciting, challenging jobs you may have already begun to explore in your pre-production and production tasks – screenwriter, artist, critic, camera operative, sound engineer – the list is long and varied. So when people ask 'Why study film?', perhaps the first response is because it's enjoyable but certainly by the time you've finished this course you will know that there's a lot more to it than that – isn't there?

Section 2: Film Language

The Reader (2008)

1: How films communicate

In many ways reading a film is very like reading a book. However, when we read a book we use our imagination to make sense from the written words – to create in our own minds pictures of characters and settings. When we read a film visual images and sound work together to convey a story. Of course we still have an individual response to what we see and many films challenge us to use our imaginations about, for example, a particular character's past, future or even present. Film directors are like authors in many ways. For example, we may be given clues in the narrative which help us to piece together the different twists and turns of a story. We may be encouraged to view the world through a particular character's eyes. The genre of a book or film will lead to a whole set of expectations about characters, narrative, style and themes. So certain kinds of books and films are created to appeal to or target particular groups of readers, e.g. Romances or Thrillers.

The openings of both films and books are important. They usually introduce us to the main characters, and set up a problem or situation that needs to be resolved in some way. Openings generally have to grab an audience's attention, to make us want to know about a particular character or situation. An author uses words written on a page, a film-maker uses technical tools which work together to communicate to the audience, in short to capture the audience's attention.

What is film language?

One of the most important aspects of your Film Studies course is to gain a clear understanding of the term 'film language' and to be able to analyse how it creates meaning and response for an audience.

By now you will be aware that there is a lot more to studying a film than simply watching with a box of popcorn in one hand and a soft drink in the other! Of course, your response to the film is very important and it is always useful or enjoyable to discuss with others how a film made you feel. But in order to fully express a detailed knowledge and understanding of films, the ways in which they communicate, and how they make you feel, you have to have a vocabulary that you can use effectively. The term vocabulary refers to the words used within a particular language. When studying film we need to know, understand and use the appropriate words to identify, describe and analyse the films we are studying. This vocabulary is known as **film language**.

'Micro' and 'macro' categories

In order to make the study of film language easier to understand it is often divided into two categories or parts. These categories are called 'micro' and 'macro'. Just as their name suggests the term 'micro' is used to refer to the technical elements of film-making. These can be analysed in short film sequences and still images. In GCSE Film Studies we group the 'micro' elements under four headings:

- Sound – including music and sound effects.
- Cinematography – the use of camera; can also include lighting and colour.
- Editing – the process of putting shots together after filming.
- Mise-en-scène – the look and positioning of all the objects and characters in a shot; can also include lighting and colour.

Although we initially look at each of these four elements separately, it is really important that we consider how they work together in a sequence in order to create meaning and response.

Mise-en-scène
Setting & props
Costume, hair & make up
Facial expressions/body language
Lighting & colour
Positioning within a frame

Sound
Diegetic (on/off screen)
Non-diegetic
Sound bridges
Parallel/contrapuntal
Ambient
Sound effects

Film language micro

Cinematography

Framing	Movement
Close up	Tracking
Extreme close up	Crane
Mid shot	Tilt
Long shot	Pan
High angle	Roll
Low angle	
Focus	

Editing

Speed	Style
Fast	Straight cut
Slow	Fade
	Dissolve
	Wipe
	Jump
	Graphic match

9

Lighting can be thought of either as part of mise-en-scène or as part of cinematography. In the film industry, lighting tends to be the responsibility of cinematographers whereas writers on film (academics and theorists) think of lighting as part of mise-en-scène – part of the shot they analyse. For GCSE Film we have followed the academics and treated lighting as part of mise-en-scène. If you go on to study A Level Film Studies, you'll find that lighting is included in the cinematography micro feature as students are likely to use lighting when filming.

The **macro elements** of film language are what we might class as the major aspects of how films are organised in order to tell stories. In this course these are studied under four headings, although again it must be stressed that all of the micro and macro elements combine to communicate to an audience and fulfil the intentions of director and screenwriter. The four macro elements are:

- Narrative – plot, viewpoint, the story and the way it is told.
- Genre – the type or category of film.
- Representation – the ways in which people, places and events are presented.
- Ideology – the different ways of seeing the world and **value systems** evident in films.

The following sections will take you through the four 'micro' and the four 'macro' elements of film language in some detail. The sequences and stills used are from films that you may have studied for Paper 1 and Paper 2. Your knowledge and understanding of how film language communicates are the key to developing a critical and investigative approach to films, the film industry, and film audiences. In short it provides you with the foundation for each area of study in this GCSE – if you can understand, discuss and respond to the ways in which all the component parts of film language combine to communicate ideas across a range of films and contexts, examination success is bound to follow.

2: Sound

In this section we will look at the ways in which sound creates meaning and response using two films, *Rabbit-Proof Fence,* and *The Boy in the Striped Pyjamas,* as examples. It doesn't matter if you are not studying these particular films for Paper 1 or 2, because the skills learnt and questions asked can be used to explore the use of sound across a whole range of other films.

Key terms

Macro elements
The overview, the big picture, the themes and issues.

Value system
The principles of right and wrong. What is accepted as important by an individual or a social group.

Baz Luhrmann creates a 'wall' of sound in *Moulin Rouge (2001)*

How do I talk about sound?

Sound is a very important part of film language. In order to analyse the use of sound in films, you will need to understand, and use the appropriate language associated with this area of study. In order to help you do this effectively we have provided you with a 'sound **terminology** tool kit' – that is a 'bank' of words, or phrases that can be used to describe sound and to evaluate how it creates meaning and response.

Sound terminology tool kit

Soundtrack	Parallel	Sound bridge
Diegetic	Soundscape	Ambient sound
Non-diegetic	Sound effects: synchronous and asynchronous	Background music
Contrapuntal		Dialogue

Diegetic sound

The the term **diegetic sound** is used to describe sound that is part of the film's world, e.g. dialogue, a dog barking or the wind blowing. The diegetic sound within a film usually creates a 'realistic' feel to the film's world. However, you should pay close attention to sound levels when thinking about how diegetic sounds create meaning and response. For example, in scene 3 from *Rabbit-Proof Fence* (07.14 – 11.40). Molly is in conversation with the man mending the fence. The **ambient sound** of birds, dogs barking and wind blowing becomes louder and much more noticeable. It creates a natural **soundscape** which suggests that everything is not as calm or as peaceful as it may first have appeared.

Non-diegetic sound

Non-diegetic sound is sound that is NOT part of the film's world. For example, background music or voice-overs. Sometimes diegetic and non-diegetic sound combine to create a particular kind of response within the audience. For example, in scene 3 from *Rabbit-Proof Fence,* the diegetic sounds mentioned above, especially the howling of the wind, combine to create a supernatural, spiritual feeling. As Grace is threatened it feels as if the whole of nature is screaming, it is on her side.

Soundtrack

The term soundtrack is used to describe the recorded sound element of a film – this includes both the diegetic and non-diegetic sound. The soundtrack contains four important elements:

- Dialogue – the human voice
- Sound effects
- Music
- Silence.

Key terms

Terminology
The words or phrases used in a particular subject

Diegetic sound
Sound that is part of the film's world, e.g. dialogue, a dog barking or the wind blowing.

Ambient sound
The sounds of a given location or space, for example a wood with leaves rustling, birds singing, waterfall splashing.

Soundscape
A sound or combination of sounds that forms or arises from a particular kind of environment.

Each element of a film's soundtrack combines or contributes to making meaning and creating response.

Dialogue

The dialogue in a film helps to create character, to tell the story, and to express the feelings and motivations of a character. 'The way you say it' is also important in terms of dialogue. For example, Tsotsi says very little throughout the film, he gives brief orders to his gang; he expresses his anger through violence. The turning point in the film happens when he visits Miriam for the last time. He knocks at the door and asks 'Can I come in?' He follows this request with 'Please'. This is an emotional scene; a lot is communicated through body language and silence, the pauses create meaning. Both characters know that a turning point has been reached. A simple 'please' and 'thank-you' uttered for the first time indicates that Tsotsi will take the baby back to its home. The dialogue, and the way it is delivered, tells us so much about his character and his role in the film.

Sound effects

Synchronous sound

These are sounds that match what we can see on screen. For example, near the beginning of *The Boy in the Striped Pyjamas* a band is playing in Bruno's house for the family's farewell party. Synchronous sounds can contribute to the realism of a film and also help to create atmosphere. For example, in scene 3 from *Rabbit-Proof Fence* (0.7.14 – 0.11.40) the camel's snorting as the girls pass its enclosure is a little disturbing as are the other 'ambient' natural noises we hear. It perhaps signals that all is not as peaceful as it might appear.

The camel, an example of asynchronous and synchronous sound: *Rabbit-Proof Fence*

Asynchronous sound

These are sound effects not matched with a visible source of sound on the screen. Off screen sound can create the impression of a three-dimensional space. It can also create a particular mood or atmosphere, for example the barking of the dogs which punctuates the action on scene 3 of *Rabbit-Proof Fence*. The dogs are not visible but their barking seeps into the shots showing Molly and the other girls playing and Molly's mother's conversation with the station manager. Their barking disturbs Molly's mother's confident assertion that Mr 'Evil' would not be able to take her Molly. It produces a tension between what is said and what we believe might happen. It raises our curiosity and expectation. In this sequence the camel's snorting also works in an asynchronous way. The camel is no longer in shot but its snorting becomes louder and more agitated, signalling the arrival of the policeman who is to take Molly and the other girls away to an internment camp.

Watch out it's behind you!

Music

Music can be as powerful as images in terms of 'pinning down' the meaning of a sequence. Background music is often used to add emotion and rhythm to a film. Sometimes it is really noticeable. On other occasions it provides us with clues about the emotions of specific characters and what might be driving their actions. It can work in parallel with what we see on the screen, creating or enhancing a romantic moment, or accentuating a frightening occurrence. It can often foreshadow a change in mood. For example **dissonant** music may be used to indicate an approaching, but not yet visible, menace or disaster.

Background music can also aid continuity and help us to link particular scenes, for example the **sound bridge** used in *The Boy in the Striped Pyjamas* (07.24 – 09.50). This sequence shows the party on Bruno's final evening in Berlin, which ends with the band playing 'Wish me luck as you wave me goodbye'. This music carries over (sound bridges) into a scene the following morning where Bruno is still playing 'fighter pilots' in the corridor, oblivious of the imminent move. The music tells us that perhaps he is going to need a deal of luck in order to adjust to his new life, but he is still firmly rooted in his imaginary play world.

Silence

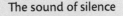

The sound of silence

Silence can have a powerful effect on the way an audience interprets or responds to a sequence. Always be aware that if there is silence accompanying the images on screen, it is there for a purpose. Often silence can create far more tension in a taut scene than the use of 'scary' music. If the silence is punctuated by a loud noise, it makes the audience jump. Silence may force the audience to concentrate on particularly important moments and can be very powerful when working in tandem with the cinematography, for example in the moments

Key terms

Dissonant
Unpleasant use of sound or notes – a lack of harmony.

Sound bridge
Sound which carries over from one scene to another often forcing the viewer to make connections between the scenes.

when hero and villain face each other before their final battle in a Superhero film. Typically, these moments work together with close-ups, to create moments of extreme tension whilst we wait for the battle to begin.

Describing sounds

Alongside your 'terminology tool kit' you will also need to have a 'bank' of words which describe the sorts of sounds that make up the soundtrack and the kinds of effect they create. You can describe music by referring to the:

- Country of origin
- Style of the music
- Instrument making the sound
- Purpose of the music.

Here are some examples of descriptive words for the genre or style of music used:

Country and Western, Rock, Blues, Hip hop, Classical, Folk, Traditional, Lament, Lullaby.

Timbre is the term for the colour of music, the sound of it. Below are just a few of the words that can be used to describe the sound music makes in film:

Loud, soft, brassy, gentle, romantic, strong, eerie, spooky, rhythmic, choppy, noisy, mellow, shrill, clear, piercing, harsh, warm, bright, heavy, light, and flat.

After identifying the genre, style, or sounds, created by the music in a sequence you will need to describe MEANING and RESPONSE. Here are some words or phrases that describe what music can do to you and for you:

Frighten, soothe, excite, relax, stimulate, calm, give a feeling of foreboding, stir your imagination, make you happy, lift your mood, lift your spirits, make you more alert, exhilarate, and bring about practically any emotion.

TASK 1

Create your own table, similar to the one below, which contains words and phrases that may be useful when analysing how music creates meaning and response in some of the films you have studied for either Paper 1 or Paper 2.

Style	Timbre	Meaning/response	Film
Traditional, lament	Sad, calm, eerie	Sweet sadness, past interacting with present	*Tsotsi*
Rock	Loud, heavy, aggressive	Non-conformity, strength	*The Wave*
Classical	Gentle, rhythmic	Calmness, innocence, unawareness of real world	*The Boy in the Striped Pyjamas*

Finally, always be aware of the multitude of relations sound can have to the images you see on screen and to the film's narrative. It can be background music, its source can be on or off screen. It can come before or after an image, linking ideas or themes.

Pick a sequence from one of your studied films. It should be one in which you think sound is particularly important. For example, the closing sequence of *The Boy in the Striped Pyjamas* or scene 3 from *Rabbit-Proof Fence*. Then consider the following questions:

● Are the sound effects artificial or natural sounding?

● Do they have an off or on screen source?

● Is sound used to link images?

● Does sound ever become more important than the images and what is the reason for this unusual strategy?

● Concentrate on dialogue and silence. Do different characters use different kinds of language – slang, dialect, profanity? Do certain characters speak through their silence?

● What kind of music is used? Is it typical of the period or place depicted? Does music **foreshadow** or **contradict** the action? How does it shape our interpretation of what we see on screen?

The questions posed in the task above should provide you with a strong framework for analysing how sound makes meaning in any sequence.

TASK 2

3: Cinematography

The term cinematography basically refers to the recording of moving images. A cinematographer films moving images. When analysing how cinematography creates meaning and response it is important to consider the choice of camera shots and camera movement. You will also need a straightforward set of key terms to describe them.

Cinematography terminology tool kit

Type of shots	Camera angles	Depth of focus	Camera movement
Close-up	Bird's-eye view	Shallow	Hand-held
Establishing shot	High angle	Deep	Pan
Extreme close-up	Low angle	Racking	Tilt
Long shot	Eye level		Track/dolly
Medium shot	Oblique/canted		Shot-reverse-shot
			Zoom

Analysing cinematography

When first describing and then analysing the ways in which cinematography communicates, it is useful to consider five important areas:

- Camera framing/type of shot
- Camera angle
- Camera movement
- Camera focus
- Shot duration.

Naming shots, exploring meaning and response

You will already have learnt that when describing different cinematic shots, different terms are used to indicate what is in the frame, how far away the camera is from the subject, and the perspective of the viewer. Each different shot has a different purpose and effect.

The key to a successful analysis is the ability to accurately name shots and then consider why these shots have been used. The term **framing** refers to the ways in which subject matter is arranged within the frame of the camera. When considering framing you should look closely at what has been included in the frame and where it has been placed.

The identification of shots, and the consideration of the importance of framing, highlights the ways that elements of film language, initially studied separately, actually work together to make meaning. Camera shots/framing plus camera angles plus depth of focus contribute to a consideration of mise-en-scène (how everything in the frame makes meaning).

Below are some examples of commonly used shots from films you may have already studied. For example, look at the still below taken from *The Wave 2008*.

Key terms

Hand-held
Hand-held cameras often denote a certain kind of gritty realism. They can make the audience feel as though they are part of a scene.

Pan
Camera movement along a horizontal axis.

Tilt
The camera is fixed and tilts upwards or downwards.

Dolly/tracking shot
The camera is placed on a moving vehicle and moves alongside the action, generally following a moving figure or object.

Zoom
Moving the camera lens in or out to bring us either closer to or further away from the action.

QUICKFIRE 1

a. What kind of shot?
b. What's in the frame and where?
c. What does the framing suggest about characters and issues?

The close-up

A close-up can also be used to magnify an object (think of how big it looks on a cinema screen) and shows the importance of things. This could be words written on paper, or (as below) the expression on someone's face. In the 'real' world we rarely get so close to someone's face so it is a very intimate shot. A film-maker may use this to make us feel extra comfortable, or extremely uncomfortable, about a character, and usually uses a zoom lens in order to get the required framing.

QUICKfire
2

a. What does this shot tell us about this character?
b. What effect does the use of shallow focus have?

The Wave: Marco finally stands up to Wenger in their final assembly

Shallow focus: Shallow focus is a function of a narrow **depth of field** and it implies that only one plane of the frame will remain sharp and clear (usually the foreground). It is typically a feature of the close-up (see above) and is often used to signal an important moment in a character's life.

The still below is taken from *Tsotsi* 2005. It shows us the exact moment when Tsotsi picks out his victim on the railway station. The shot used is an extreme version of the close-up. The **extreme close-up** generally magnifies what we might actually see. So, it may only show the mouth or eyes with no background detail whatsoever. This is a very artificial shot, and can be used for dramatic effect. Note how lighting accentuates Tsotsi's eyes – he is a dark character and he is thinking dark thoughts. (For a more detailed analysis of the shot and the way it relates to our 'reading' of this character, see Section 4: Topic 5, *Tsotsi* 'characters, themes and issues').

Key terms

Shallow focus
A function of a narrow depth of field and it implies that only one plane of the frame will remain sharp and clear (usually the foreground).

Depth of field
The term used to describe the area in focus within the frame.

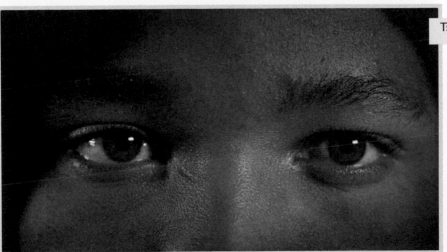

Tsotsi spots his victim

Lex Luther threatens Superman:
Superman Returns 2006

The long shot

You may have difficulty determining what a **long shot** is. Don't worry, this is a common problem with no precise answer. Generally, however, it contains a complete view of the characters, so viewers can see their costumes and perhaps recognise the relationships between them. Long shots often give us background to look at as well as the action. Sometimes this is important to the character. The still above shows Luther against the petrified landscape where he says he is going to live. It is a cold, dark, unforgiving landscape reflecting Luther's own personality.

Gotham City – a typical Metropolis
Batman Begins 2005

Describe a typical establishing shot for a Superhero movie.

Establishing shot/extreme long shot

This is a shot, usually from a distance, that shows us where we are. Often used at the beginning of a film to suggest where the story takes place. When the extreme long shot is used in this way it is called an establishing shot – it simply establishes where the action is taking place and often what period it is set in.

Camera angles

When we talk about camera angles we refer to the relationship between the camera and the object being photographed. The angle used creates particular meanings and responses, it gives emotional information to an audience, and influences their reaction to the character or object in shot.

High angle and low angle shots

Spiderman 3: Gwen's fall from the high rise from high angle and low angle – both pretty scary?

For a **high angle shot** the camera is elevated above the action to give a general overview. High angles make the object photographed seem smaller and less significant (or scary). The object or character often gets swallowed up by their setting – they become part of a wider picture.

For a **low angle shot** the camera is placed below the action, increasing the feeling of height in terms of characters and structures (typically buildings). In the shots above, both high and low angle shots create a sense of fear and tension – we see how far Gwen has to fall and then how precarious her hold on the ledge is.

Low angles help give a sense of confusion to a viewer, of powerlessness within the action of a scene. The background of a low angle shot will tend to be just sky or ceiling, the lack of detail about the setting adding to the disorientation of the viewer. The added height of the object may make it inspire fear and insecurity in the audience.

Spiderman 3: The Sandman cometh

Exam tip

Another reminder that the identification of a particular camera angle is only the first step in your analysis. First identify then explore how it affects your reaction to the character or object in shot.

Key terms

High angle shot
The camera is elevated above the action to give a general overview. High angles make the object photographed seem smaller, and less significant.

Low angle shot
The camera is placed below the action, increasing the feeling of height in terms of characters and structures.

Bird's-eye view
A camera shot that shows a scene from directly overhead, a very unnatural and strange angle.

Eye-level shot
This shot involves positioning the camera as though it is a human actually observing a scene, usually around 5–6 feet off the ground.

Oblique/canted angle
The camera is tilted (not placed horizontal to floor level), to suggest imbalance, transition and instability.

Quickfire 4

a. Name the shot.
b. What effect does it have on the audience?

It is important to note that each specific angle can create different kinds of meaning. For example, the **bird's-eye view** shows a scene from directly overhead, a very unnatural and strange angle.

Superman 3: tiny people with large heads?

Quickfire 5

Choose a camera angle for each of the following situations:

a. The audience needs to see the world through a child's eyes.

b. A Superhero is threatened by a huge monster.

c. A female is about to fall from a collapsing building.

d. Superman is flying over Metropolis looking down at the cityscape.

e. Batman is slowly regaining consciousness after being drugged by an arch enemy.

Familiar objects viewed from this angle might seem totally unrecognisable at first. This shot does, however, put the audience in a god-like position, looking down on the action. People can be made to look insignificant, ant-like, part of a wider scheme of things.

The **eye-level shot** involves positioning the camera as though it is a human actually observing a scene, usually around 5–6 feet off the ground. However, when the director wants the narrative of a film to seem to be told through, for example, a young person's eyes (as in *The Boy in the Striped Pyjamas*) the camera will be positioned much lower.

In terms of making meaning the **oblique/canted angle** is interesting, look out for it in your Superhero films, it's often used just as the Superhero is 'coming to' after being drugged or knocked unconscious. The camera is tilted (not placed horizontal to floor level), to suggest imbalance, transition and instability. This technique often suggests the character's physical or mental state – we see the world through their eyes. A hand-held camera is often used for this.

Task 3

Create a revision scrapbook document on your computer which focuses on the films you have studied for Paper 1 and Paper 2. Research stills from these films, then copy, cut and paste them into your scrapbook. Write a short analysis under each still which identifies shot and/or angle and explores how they create meaning and response.

Camera movement

When considering how meaning is made you should also be clear about the various types of camera movement and the effect they create. There are seven basic methods shown in the chart on page 21. As part of your revision process, copy and complete the chart, the first two movements are completed for you but you may wish to add examples of their use from your own study films.

Type of movement	How it is created	Effect
Zoom	Camera on tripod using a special zoom lens	A video zoom lens can change the position of the audience, either very quickly (a smash zoom) or slowly. Zoom lenses give the impression of movement and excitement in a scene.
Tilt	Camera on tripod scans a scene vertically	Often used to reveal the size of a creature, character or building, e.g. Godzilla revealed feet first.
Dolly/tracking		
Hand-held camera		
Crane shot		
Pan		
Aerial shot		

Key Term

Aerial shot
A variation of a crane shot, usually taken from a helicopter. This is often used at the beginning of a film in order to establish setting and movement.

4: Editing

Put simply, editing is the process of joining one shot with another. However, as you've already learnt, film language is sophisticated, not simple! And editing is often seen as the most important, complex and creative element of film language. How shots are joined and the order in which they are placed affect the ways in which we 'read' what is on the screen. For example, shots can be placed together so one

event follows logically from the next. We 'read' shots in conjunction with other shots; audiences work hard to link shots logically together. The most common way of joining one shot with another is **continuity editing,** a process whereby we are hardly aware of one shot moving to another. Continuity editing is much like a good toupee 'it's hard to see the joins'.

Key terms

Continuity editing
Editing that is 'invisible' producing a seamless, clear narrative.

Straight cut
A smooth transition from one shot to another.

Fade
A fade signals a movement in time and/or space in a sequence. There are usually two types of fade – a fade to white, or a fade to black. Both feature a smooth, gradual transition from a normal image to either a completely white or black screen.

Dissolve
A transition which involves one image being slowly brought in beneath another one.

Editing terminology tool kit

Type of edit	Speed of editing	Style of editing
Straight cut	Fast	Continuity
Fade	Slow	Graphic matching
Dissolve	Rhythm and pace	Cross-cutting
Wipe cut		Elliptical
Jump cut		Montage

When revising editing and thinking about the ways in which they create meaning and response, you should consider three major elements: the type of edit, the speed of editing and the style of editing.

Types of edit

The most commonly used type of edit is the **straight cut**. The use of the straight cut/continuity editing creates a sense of realism within a film. The audience does not have its attention drawn to the way the story is told.

Unlike the straight cut **fades** and **dissolves** are meant to be noticed because they conventionally carry particular meanings. Typically a fade signals a movement in time and/or space in a sequence. There are usually two types of fade – a fade to white, or a fade to black. Both feature a smooth, gradual transition from a normal image to either a completely white or black screen (fade out), or vice versa (fade in). Typically the black screen connotes 'darkness' in terms of the themes or action.

Exam tip

If a sequence you are analysing uses straight cuts/continuity editing, don't think there is nothing to say! You should consider how effectively they draw you into a scene, create a sense of realism or encourage an emotional involvement with characters and situations.

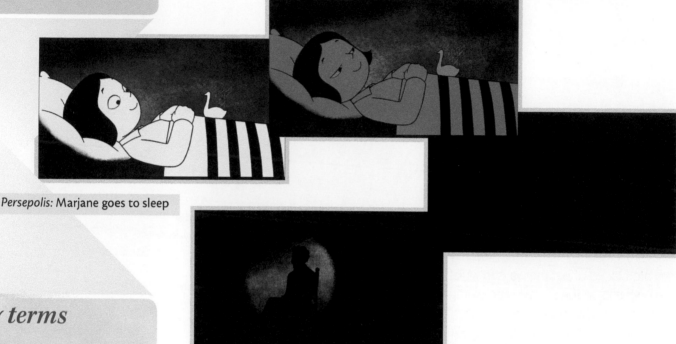

Persepolis: Marjane goes to sleep

For example, the fade to black above shows Marjane smiling as she falls asleep. Her Uncle Anoosh has given her a swan made of bread that he made in prison. She is happy after finding out that he was a 'hero' and knowing that he believes that in Iran, 'everything eventually will turn out fine'. As she sleeps there is a fade to black. We assume that time has passed and the fade in reveals an **iris** shot of Uncle Anoosh in silhouette as he talks of his disillusionment with the Iranian regime and the terrible things were happening in Iran.

Wipes and jump cuts

A **jump cut** is rapid, jerky transition from one frame to the next. It may disrupt the flow of time, or movement, within a scene, or make an abrupt transition from one scene to another. Jump cuts are typically used to unsettle the audience and/or to create moments of shock. A **wipe** is a transition between shots in which a line passes across the screen, eliminating or 'wiping out' the first shot as it goes and replacing it with the next one. It is typically used in trailers or action/adventure films. It often suggests a direct connection between the two images.

Key terms

Iris
A technique used to show an image in only one small round area of the screen. It can be used either as a transitional device, or as a way of focusing attention on a specific part of a scene without reducing the scene in size.

Jump cut
A fast transition designed to bring something to the audience's attention suddenly.

Wipe
A transition between shots in which a line passes across the screen, eliminating or 'wiping out' the first shot as it goes and replacing it with the next one.

Speed of editing

Fast and slow

The speed of editing is important. It can create a particular emotional effect within the audience. It can also help to speed up or slow down time. It can affect what we think we are seeing on screen.

Watch out! Here comes the Batmobile! *Batman Begins 2005*

Key terms

Montage
A film editing technique in which a series of short shots are edited into a sequence to condense space, time and information.

Rhythm
The regularity of sounds, series of shots, and movements within the shots.

Pace
The speed and rate of sounds, series of shots, and movements within the shots.

Shot duration

The speed of a sequence is determined by the length (in terms of time) of each shot. The decision to extend a shot can be as significant as the decision to cut it. Editing can affect the experience of time in the cinema by creating a gap between screen time and diegetic time (**montage** editing) or by establishing a fast or slow rhythm for the scene. In general, modern films feature relatively fast editing. Shots above one minute are referred to as a long take.

Exam tip

When studying a sequence, note down where the shots become shorter or noticeably longer. Analyse how and why the action is speeding up or slowing down at these points.

Rhythm and pace

The speed of shots affects the rhythm and pace of a film sequence. When we talk about **rhythm** and **pace** we need to consider the rate and regularity of sounds, series of shots, and movements within the shots. Rhythm is one of the essential features of a film, because it contributes to its mood and overall impression on the audience. It is also one of the hardest areas to analyse as it is achieved through the combination of mise-en-scène, cinematography, sound and editing. For example, in the final sequence of *The Boy in the Striped Pyjamas* all of these elements combine to create a pace and rhythm which carries the audience headlong into the film's powerful climax.

A director wishes to edit the final sequence of a Superhero movie. Briefly describe the sequence and identify how it might be edited in order to build up to an exciting climax.

TASK 4

Style

Generally when talking about style, we refer to the 'look' of the film. The 'look' of a film isn't just about cinematography, editing is also key. For example, you may notice that there is a strong visual similarity between shots. This technique, known as **graphic matching**, encourages the audience to make connections between two shots. A classic example is the graphic match in the shower sequence in *Psycho*: a slowly spiralling close-up of Marian's eye dissolves into a close-up of the blood spiralling down the shower drain.

A film-maker may make an effective use of **ellipses.** This term refers to shot **transitions** which omit parts of the story that are not significant, leaving the audience to 'fill in the gaps' in time and/or space. For instance, there would be no point in showing a scene that involves a character walking to the door to answer it unless it highlighted some important point. Elliptical editing also enables the film-maker to cut out long periods of time. Jeunet uses this technique effectively in *Amelie*. The period during which she grows from a child to a woman is shown in a brief, speeded-up sequence showing the seasons rush by and Amelie's abandoned Teddy bear. Amelie's growing up years are not important, her quirky personality has been established in the opening sequences and it is how she interacts with the world as an adult that forms the core of the narrative.

Amelie grows from child to woman as the seasons pass

Cross-cutting is also important in terms of style and the creation of meaning and response. This is editing that alternates shots of two or more lines of action occurring in different places, usually simultaneously. For example, the final sequence of *The Boy in the Striped Pyjamas* relies heavily on cross-cutting between at least three different **spheres of action.** It begins with Bruno entering the camp. His experiences in the camp are intercut with scenes from his house showing the growing realisation amongst the family that he is missing. From there cross-cutting allows us to follow Bruno's journey, father's pursuit party and mother with Gretyl who follow some minutes later. The use of this technique allows the audience to engage with the emotions of each set of characters.

Gretyl and mother arrive at the perimeter fence

CROSS-CUT TO:

Bruno and Shmuel stripped for their shower

CROSS-CUT TO:

Father's panic rises as he searches the hut for Bruno

Task 5

Write an analysis of editing in a key sequence from your focus film for Paper 2 (Film Outside Hollywood). You should include a consideration of each of the major areas of editing: speed, type and style.

25

5: Mise-en-scène

Mise-en-scène terminology tool kit

Lighting	Positioning	Meaning	Style
High key	Foreground	Connotation	Mood
Low key	Background	Denotation	Colour palette
Top	Centre frame		Stylised
Back			

Every element of a visual image can carry meaning. What is in the **frame** of a picture – the mise-en-scène – gives us a lot of information which we use to help us understand the film. So when analysing mise-en-scène there are several aspects that you need to consider all at once. These are:

- **Setting**
- Props and costume
- Character positioning within the frame
- Body language, expression and movement
- Lighting and colour.

Lighting and colour

'There is a lot of natural lighting in the sequence I am analysing because the setting is outside and the weather is good.'

The sentence above, written by a student, highlights a common problem when considering lighting in a sequence. In reality most film-making needs lights. You may think that if a film-maker wants a film to look natural, they just need to turn up on location, set up the camera and shoot. You couldn't be more wrong! If you could visit a film set you would be amazed by just how bright film lights are. Lights are necessary because film does not respond to light the same way our eyes do. There is no way you can do an exterior night shoot without lights, even if there is a full moon. This means that to make a scene look natural, ironically, you must use enough lights. Lighting also creates **mood**. The two main ways of describing lighting techniques are **high key** and **low key lighting**. High key lighting is used to refer to a scene that utilises several lights in order to create a bright, clear environment. The **key light** is the main light used and **filler lights** are used to achieve levels of brightness and eliminate shadows. Low key lighting uses fewer filler lights in order to create distinctive areas of light and shadow.

Film-makers often use lighting to create a heightened interpretation of reality; in other words, films that seem 'more real than real'. This is simply a way of saying that they are not bland (think about the vibrancy of colours in Spiderman's world, or the dark, gothic world that Batman inhabits). Both films present an enhanced view of 'reality' which involves using highly **stylised** lighting.

Exam tip

Always consider how all these elements work together to create meaning and response. Mise-en-scène refers to the complete image shown in the frame.

Key terms

Top lighting
When the upper areas of a subject are lit (outlined) by a source generating from above it.

Back lighting
Adds a sense of depth to shots. In film, the background light is usually of lower intensity. More than one light could be used to light uniformly a background or alternatively to highlight points of interest.

Foreground
The front of the frame.

Frame
The edges of the picture, and what is contained within the space they surround.

Setting
The place, time and scenery of a story.

Key terms

Mood
A particular kind of atmosphere.

High key lighting
The use of several lights in order to create a bright, clear environment.

Low key lighting
This uses fewer filler lights in order to create distinctive areas of light and shadow.

Key light
This the main light used in a lighting plan.

Filler lights
These are used to achieve levels of brightness and eliminate shadows.

Stylised
A distinctive or elaborate look.

What kinds of lighting are used in the still from *Iron Man*? What effects are created?

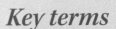

Just how big is that? Pepper Potts in *Iron Man*

Key terms

Colour palette
The assortment or range of colours used by the film-maker.

Gothic horror
Atmospheric horror based on supernatural creatures such as ghosts coming back from the dead to seek revenge.

Carlos explores the basement room in *The Devil's Backbone 2001*

Look carefully at the ways in which Del Toro uses lighting in the still on the left. What kind of lighting is used in this still?

The way in which a film-maker uses colour and lighting can impact on most other elements of mise-en-scène. It can be an integral part of costume props and setting. Film-makers will have a clear sense of the way in which they want the colour to work in a scene, it carries meaning and impacts on our emotions. If we look again at the still above, the main light source appears to be coming from a window at the back of the frame, this picks out a large pool of water. A back light casts the boy's own shadow in front as he moves towards the pool. The colours used range from silver grey, through dark blues towards black. This **colour palette** is often associated with the **Gothic horror** genre and it combines with **setting** (a dark, cavernous place with vaulted roof) to create a whole set of expectations within the audience.

Extend the consideration of lighting and colour in *'Carlos explores the basement room'* to include character positioning in the frame, body language, expression, movement, props and costume.

27

Del Toro also uses a strong amber palette in *The Devil's Backbone*. Outside, the strong amber light appears to come from the sun but the narrative contains several references to 'an insect trapped in amber', even in the classroom – see still below – the amber light dominates, emphasising a key theme of entrapment in the film. So colour can work symbolically combining with key themes to affect the way we read specific sequences.

The Devil's Backbone: Carmen teaches the boys about prehistoric creatures

Setting

The set design or choice of location should always be considered when analysing mise-en-scène. In terms of the Superhero genre, it allows film-makers to impress audiences with huge crowds, iconic buildings, urban or exotic landscapes. These also provide narrative opportunities – the Superhero must protect recognisable environments from those characters with evil intent. They also offer the opportunity to use special effects and create **spectacle** when attacked. On another level they can underline key issues. In the opening of *Tsotsi*, *Ratcatcher* and *Yasmin* the key issues of poverty and racism are clearly underlined by the poverty of environment revealed through location.

Glasgow in the 1970s: The setting for *Ratcatcher*

Working together: props, costume, body language, framing

Although often listed separately, all of the above typically work together to create meaning. When analysing mise-en-scène it is useful to think about denotation and connotation. **Denotation** refers to what we see on the screen. **Connotation** refers to the meaning we may associate with what we see. Compare the extracts below from two student analyses of mise-en-scène in the cellar scene from *The Devil's Backbone* (see 'Carlos explores the basement' still).

1 Carlos has short dark brown hair. He is wearing blue and white striped pyjamas. The basement is dark and empty, there is a pool at the back of it. Lots of large pots stand up against the wall and wooden things hang from the ceiling.

2 It is dark, Carlos has bare feet and is wearing his pyjamas. His costume makes him seem small and vulnerable as he explores the huge, dark cellar with its high ceilings. The cellar feels like a torture chamber with wooden structures hanging from the walls and yet Carlos strides purposefully towards the pool. Although he is small and vulnerable his curiosity is stronger than his fear.

Both answers are well written. Student 1 describes what is seen – denotation. Student 2 describes and then analyses – she considers denotation and connotation. She also looks at mise-en-scène as a whole, taking in aspects of body language, costume and setting.

It is useful to consider where a character is positioned in the frame alongside body language and costume.

Ratcatcher: James explores one of the new houses on the outskirts of Glasgow

In this beautiful shot we see James in the foreground, centre frame looking out through the glassless window of a house on a new housing estate outside Glasgow. We can just make out the kitchen sink in the darkness, all of the light appears to come from the open window, which creates a 'picture frame' for the vibrant colours of the cornfield and the sky above it. James has stopped and is gazing at the window, as if it is a picture in an art gallery. He is wearing dark clothes which melt into the darkness of the room but his head is framed by the light.

Exam tip

Again don't try to find meaning where there is none. For example, costume can be highly significant or symbolic, e.g. *Superman* – it may simply be typical for that character, e.g. Lois Lane. Props can be significant and carry meaning – Miriam's glass mobiles in *Tsotsi*, or be simply functional – the table and chairs in her room.

QUICKFire
9

What does the mise-en-scène suggest that James is thinking?

6: The 'macro' elements of film language

What are they?

When we talk about the 'macro' elements of film language we are referring to the major aspects of how films tell stories. The 'micro' elements are the finer details. As with the study of English language or literature we consider specific areas separately at first in order to focus more carefully on them. However, in any analysis we should come back to the ways in which all the elements combine to create meaning – in short to create a language. The specification identifies the 'macro' elements of film language as:

- Genre
- Narrative.

In terms of genre you should be able to identify **genre codes and conventions** and understand the ways in which themes, issues, narrative, plot, iconography and characters are typically used within a group or category of films. The study of typicality also includes a consideration of 'micro' elements including mise-en-scène, cinematography, editing and sound (style).

Spiderman 2 poster: genre conventions selling the movie

Genre study also involves the study of the relationship between genre, industry and audiences. The ways in which audiences respond to particular genres, the popularity of particular genres at different points in time is really important to the film industry. Often genre is one of the key factors in determining whether a film will get made or not. Its importance in terms of production, distribution and exhibition should not be underestimated.

The term narrative refers to the way the story of a film is told as well as the story itself. Your study of narrative should include:

- Narrative structure – the order in which the film's action takes place and the role of editing in that structure.
- Character functions – the role of central character, supporting characters, heroes and villains.
- Locations and settings – their role in narrative construction.
- Narrative theory – for example, binary oppositions, equilibrium and disequilibrium, open and closed narratives.

The study of genre and narrative is closely connected or interlinked with issues of representation and ideology. Representation refers to the ways in which films present information about different social groups. It also involves looking carefully at the ways in which the 'micro' elements of film language convey this information. Your study of representation should include a consideration of:

- How age, gender, ethnicity and disability are presented in films.
- The role of stereotypes and **stock characters**.
- The ways in which different groups of people and their beliefs are shown.

The final 'macro' area of study is ideology. The term ideology refers to a way of seeing the world; for example, ideas, values and beliefs that are common to a specific group of people. When considering ideology you should think about:

- How representations convey different points of view and reflect different ways of seeing the world.
- The value systems evident in the films you have studied.

7: Genre

Genre study is a key way of looking at how films are analysed, how they are made, and how they are received by audiences. You will have explored the importance of genre during your work on the Superhero genre. Paper 1 is designed to assess your knowledge and understanding of genre conventions across a range of films. It also examines your grasp of its relationship with industry and audiences. Your controlled assessment work should also evidence a creative understanding of the ways in which producers and audiences use and respond to genre.

It highlights the close relationship between audience and industry. It is constantly changing, combining familiar and unexpected 'ingredients'.

Audiences know what to expect. Genre influences which films they choose to see.

Genre films offer a set of rules and vocabulary which organise meaning and allow **comparative study**.

Why is genre important?

It provides a 'safety net' for producers because of its strong relationship with audiences. This minimises the risk of financial failure.

It provides a set of familiar characteristics or a formula recognised by audiences.

It can offer relatively simple solutions to complex problems providing the audience with comfort and reassurance.

Genre study does NOT aim to identify every film as belonging to a specific genre. If you try do this you will quickly discover that all films share generic characteristics. *Superman* may contain all of your 'list of ingredients' for a Superhero film but it also contains Romance, Action, Fantasy and so on.

Genre is important because it allows us to compare a whole group of films, to look for similarities, to identify differences, to note how they have changed over time, to explore why these changes have happened, and to consider what they might say about a society at a particular point in history.

How do we identify genre?

Key terms

Recurring features
Features repeated throughout a film.

Convention
The 'rules' of the genre – micro and macro aspects the audience expect when considering a named genre.

Given that all films are, to some extent, cross-generic, how do we decide which films sit most easily under a particular genre heading? Perhaps the best way is look for **recurring features**, elements of film language that are repeated across a range of films, ingredients that when mixed together make up a particular kind of genre 'cake'.

So here are your first six typical ingredients, the **conventions** you initially consider when studying genre.

	Horror genre	Superhero genre	Romance genre
Setting	Dark cellars, old castles. Spirits and ghosts		
Characters	Vampires, vampire slayers, vulnerable females		
Narrative/plot	A ghostly being comes back from the past seeking revenge. It can only be stopped by one man		
Props/significant objects	Crucifix, bible, knives, gravestones		
Themes and issues	Redemption, revenge, fear of the unknown		
Style	Low key lighting creating areas of shadow. Jump cuts creating a sense of shock/ disorientation.		

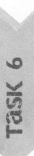

TASK 6

Copy and complete the table by filling in the Superhero and Romance genre boxes.

Section 3 'The Superhero genre' will take you through each of the six conventions above in some detail. It will also consider stylistic or visual conventions. The 'look' of a film is important. It is often a key factor in the identification of genre. Fast editing, slow motion and special effects typify the Superhero movie. Settings, props, narrative and characters, may help us to identify the Horror genre in *The Devil's Backbone* but these also combine with the use of mise-en-scène and editing to create a whole set of expectations within the audience. *Amelie* is a romance; Jeunet combines high key

Amelie: a fairy-tale romance

lighting with a palette of warm reds and greens. He has a distinct visual style but the bright colours and use of high key lighting are typical of many of romantic films made both in and outside Hollywood.

Some genres stand out because they deal with particular themes and issues. The Superhero genre deals with revenge, redemption, truth and justice in an 'all-American' way. Gothic horror films (*The Devil's Backbone)* also deal with revenge and redemption but are stylistically quite different. All of the films in your Films Outside Hollywood list have a young person at the heart of their narratives but in terms of style they are quite different. Style can also vary within genres; for example, the social realism of *Rabbit-Proof Fence* is stylistically very different to that of *Ratcatcher.*

You should also consider the use of **iconography** in your study of genre. Iconography refers to recurring symbols that carry meaning from film to film. It can be an object or a setting – the outline of a crucifix where it had once hung on a classroom wall could symbolise an impoverished or godless environment (see still in mise-en-scène section: *The Devil's Backbone*). The destruction of the Statue of Liberty symbolises a threat to the 'American values' of freedom and democracy. Even stars can become iconic, e.g. Christopher Reeves as a 'Superman'.

Audience and industry

Genre is a great way of creating a pathway into a film for audiences. Once a particular genre has been signalled there is so much a film-maker can leave out because we are already able to fill in the gaps. For example, as soon as we identify Tsotsi as a young gangster, a thug, in the opening sequence, we suspect he will ultimately have to pay for his crimes. Genre can also work in a different way, by confounding our expectations. *Spiderman 3* caused quite a lot of controversy when it was first released because it played with our perceptions of what a Superhero should be. Peter Parker had become obsessed by his Spiderman image and his '**alter-ego**' takes over. What the audience was presented with was an immoral, vain, selfish, protagonist. However, producers know just how far to go in terms of variation, and the resolution saw Spiderman/Peter Parker, returning to 'good old American values' once more.

Audiences expect the familiar but demand new variations. Film-makers have to be careful when negotiating this tension between similarity and difference. We want something new but also need the reassurance that those things which give us pleasure are not lost. Genre allows the audience to choose, read narrative clues, predict and compare films. It provides the industry with a simple, powerful way of selling films to a target audience. In order to maintain audience popularity, genre must be seen to be fresh and appealing. So it is constantly changing, often looking to innovative film-makers such as Tim Burton, Chris Nolan or Guillermo Del Toro, to refresh existing genres by putting their own distinctive stamp on them.

Many Superheroes have an alter ego. Name as many as you can and describe the differences between the characters' first and second personalities.

8: Narrative

Narrative terminology tool kit

Narrative structure	Narrative viewpoint	Narrative theory
Flashback	Narrator	Enigma codes
Flashforward	Voice-over	Character types
Cyclical	Restricted viewpoint	Character functions
Linear	Omniscient viewpoint	Binary oppositions
Chronological	Diegesis	
Cause and effect		

When we study narrative it is important to remember that we must think about the way in which the story of the film is told, as well as the story itself. Narrative structure is about two things: the content of a story and the form used to tell the story.

It's the way film stories are told. How meaning is constructed to achieve audience understanding.

It groups events into cause and effect – action and event.

It allows a consideration of narrative voice – whose story is told and from whose perspective.

Why study narrative?

It organises time and space.

It involves analysing everything you hear or see (the plot) and those film events that are not necessarily shown but may be inferred (the story).

Story and plot

The story of a film includes all the events that are not shown but have been inferred. For example, we know that in *Tsotsi* Miriam's husband is dead but we are not shown exactly what has happened to him.

When we consider plot we analyse everything we can hear or see. We focus on 'how' and 'when':

1. How and when is the major conflict story set up?

2. How and when are particular characters introduced?

3. How is the story moved along so that characters must face the central conflict?

4. How and when does the major conflict reach its climax?

5. How and when are the major conflicts resolved?

Story and plot are slightly different ways of analysing a film; they refer to different ways in which meaning is made. Story determines key conflicts, characters, setting and events. Plot is about how and when key conflicts are set up and perhaps resolved. When studying Hollywood films you may have noticed that whilst stories may change, plot structure remains almost identical. Your study of Films Outside Hollywood may have allowed an exploration of more varied plot structures especially in terms of resolution, e.g. *Rabbit-Proof Fence*, *Ratcatcher*, *The Wave* and *Persepolis*.

No resolution? Wenger is taken away in a police car at the end of *The Wave*

> ## Exam tip
> Narrative refers to the way a story is told, so consider audience positioning. Examine why you sympathise with a character. Are you given more information about them? How do elements of film language encourage you to see the world from a particular character's perspective?

Task 7

1. Pick a film from your Paper 1 study and then answer 'How' questions 1–5 (on page 34) referring to your study film.

2. Repeat the process focusing on your Paper 2 study film.

3. Note down the differences and similarities in terms of plot structure for each film.

Narrative structure

The term 'narrative structure' refers to the ways in which all the parts of a film are put together and organised. Stories in films aren't always told in the order they happen. Film-makers can move us backwards and forwards in time, they can show us events from different characters' points of view. Different techniques can be used to show us different parts of a story. In *Tsotsi* the central character's past is revealed through a series of **flashbacks**, these are interspersed with the story of Tsotsi's attempts to look after Baby David. The flashbacks are timed to reveal more and more of Tsotsi's past and to elicit audience sympathy. As our understanding of what has affected his previous actions grows, our initial response to this 'thug' changes.

The most commonly used narrative structures are:

● Cyclical – a narrative that is often accompanied by voice-overs and begins at the end using one or a series of flashbacks to construct the whole narrative, Finally returning to where it began in time and space, e.g. *Saving Private Ryan*.

● Linear – the most simple and commonly used narrative structure. The story is told **chronologically**. Films with a linear structure typically organise stories into a **cause and effect** pattern where the consequences of one action lead on to something else.

> ## Key terms
>
> **Flashback**
> Narrative device in which the action is interrupted by scenes representing a character's memory of events experienced before the time of the action.
>
> **Flashforward**
> The opposite of flashback: future events (or events imagined by a character) are shown.
>
> **Chronologically**
> A sequence of events arranged in order of occurrence.
>
> **Cause and effect**
> Cause is the specific action a person does which leads to an effect or consequence of the action. The effect of that action may be good or bad and may be determined by the cause.

35

- Episodic – in general, an episodic narrative is a story that is broken up into events, or episodes that are somehow connected. Often the connections are not fully apparent until near the end of the story.

Narrative viewpoint

When considering audience response to a film it is important to note from which viewpoint we are asked to see the story. A **narrator/voice-over** can have a huge impact by giving us 'insider information' on particular characters. Cinematography can connect us with characters and their situations. For example, in *The Boy in the Striped Pyjamas,* a connection is encouraged by using frequent camera shots at Bruno's eye level, so we see the world through his eyes.

Film-makers can offer a **restricted narrative** viewpoint. This means we only get to know what the character knows and accompany him through the action, encountering/overcoming obstacles almost 'side-by-side'. This technique is used in *The Devil's Backbone* when we explore the mysteries locked up within the orphanage alongside Carlos.

Some films offer a 'God-like', or **omniscient** perspective of the film's **diegesis.** This allows us to know more than the main protagonists, we see events that they don't, and are allowed access to important narrative information. This can create a feeling of tension and/or suspense within the audience as we know what dangers lie ahead but are powerless to influence them.

Narrative theory

Firstly a word of warning – BE VERY, VERY CAREFUL when referring to narrative theory. This can be helpful, if used wisely, but it can also lead you away from that all-important personal response to the various elements of film language.

Vladimir Propp: this theorist studied Russian folk stories in the 1920s and was able to identify particular character types. He then looked at the **function** that each character served within the narrative. His theories were later used when analysing films and have been useful in terms of a consideration of how little information audiences need in order to identify particular character types, and then predict their actions, motivations, and relationships with other characters. Identifying a character, for example as 'the hero', can be helpful, especially if you then go on to analyse whether it affects your response to that character. Does it allow you to predict actions, motivations, or possible relationships? Helpful, too, to consider what effect it may have had on your viewing experience, if the expectations you had were in some way undermined. However, just identifying a character type and giving Propp's description of character functions does not enrich your analysis at all and in an exam context precious words/time may be wasted.

Likewise with **Todorov, Levi-Strauss and Barthes** – use with care and they can lead you towards a thoughtful analysis. Barthes' focus upon **enigma codes** is a useful way of thinking about audience and how a film maintains our interest. Barthes looked at the little puzzles which an audience is asked to solve throughout the plot, how these make us work hard, and give us pleasure. In the context of *Rabbit-Proof Fence*, an early enigma or puzzle centres around the reasons for taking Grace, Molly and Daisy away from their families. Later we wonder why Moodoo, the Aboriginal tracker, is willing to hunt for the escaped girls, and then why the servant in the farmhouse is so frightened of the farmer. These smaller enigmas work with the big enigma, 'Will the girls survive the 1,000 mile journey back to their home?' in order to keep our interest and add to our enjoyment of the film.

Levi-Strauss looked at the way meaning is made through **binary oppositions** – how exciting narratives are created through the conflict between two sides, or qualities, that are opposites. This may be a good way into your study of the Superhero genre – how typical narratives are created by binary oppositions such as: good vs evil, Superhero vs Supervillain, selflessness vs greed, democracy vs dictatorship. Just remember that it is not enough to simply identify the binary oppositions, you must explore how they create meaning and response – why they are important.

Todorov focused on the ways in which narratives were structured. He identified different stages, e.g. beginnings, middles or ends, where important information or messages are conveyed. For example, at the end we typically expect the villain to be punished and the forces of good in a society to win out. This may not be true in 'real life' but is presented in many of the films we watch.

Narrative time and space

There is a close relationship between the 'micro' elements of film language, cinematography and editing and the manipulation of time and space within a film. Parallel editing can allow the audience to follow two different 'spheres of action' featuring different characters in different places, at the same time. You will have already focused on how this works in the final sequence of *The Boy in the Striped Pyjamas* in the 'micro' editing section. Cinematography can also stretch time by using slow motion, or speed it up with fast editing. We accept the gaps in narrative time (ellipsis) – a film may cover several weeks, months, years or centuries in 90 minutes. We can move across continents in a few seconds.

Exam tip

When considering narrative think carefully about how your study films deal with time and space. It is an important way of making meaning.

9: Representation

Representation is an important concept in Film Studies as it refers to how films relay information about social groups. It also allows us to think about how our beliefs and culture affect the ways in which we see the world.

It refers to the negative and positive aspects of stereotyping

It allows a consideration of how much of the world is represented to us through the media

Why study representation?

Looks at how films communicate particular messages

Involves an analysis of the relationship between representation and genre

Focuses on the ways in which audiences read representation differently

Representation terminology tool kit

Generic types	Readings	Social groupings
Archetypes	Preferred	Culture, Social class
Stereotypes	Negotiated	Ethnicity, Age
1- , 2- or 3-dimensional characters	Oppositional	Gender, Disability

Key terms

Decode
To convert a coded message in order to examine its meaning.

Preferred reading
Where a spectator understands and largely agrees with the messages/values evident in a film.

Negotiated reading
Where a spectator agrees with some messages and values but not all.

Oppositional reading
Where spectator disagrees/dislikes the film's messages and values.

Key terms

One-dimensional character
An undeveloped, minor character only briefly shown.

Two-dimensional character
Features more at forefront of the story but has no complexity or depth, e.g. purely good or bad.

Three-dimensional character
Showing all the complexity of a real person, e.g. not entirely good or bad.

Generic types
A certain personality or type of character seen repeatedly in a particular genre.

Stereotypical
A simplistic way of representing people, places or groups.

Archetype
An easily recognised representation of a character that has been used for a long time.

Preferred, negotiated and oppositional readings

We all **decode** representations according to our own life experience, where we've lived, how old we are and what we may have read or seen in the media. Other elements, for example our social class, can also come into play. So producers may assume that everybody responds to film in the same way and construct representations accordingly, but clearly that is a questionable assumption. Everybody has a personal response to a film; this may be linked to our social or cultural background, but we all have a distinctive, individual point-of-view. This response is referred to as a 'reading' in Film Studies.

If your reaction to the film is broadly similar to others who have seen it and you understand the points that the film-maker is trying to get across, you are said to have a '**preferred reading**' of the film. If you agree with some of the film-maker's points but not others, then you are giving a '**negotiated reading**'. If you really disliked the film and all it stands for you have an '**oppositional reading**'. Below are excerpts from three responses to the final question on Paper 2:

1. 'Tsotsi moved me because it made me see that life is like a game of chance — if we are dealt a poor hand we may struggle to do the right thing.'

2. 'I understand how difficult Tsotsi's life must have been so I do feel sorry for him, but we all know right from wrong so he should not have acted in the way he did.'

3. 'Tsotsi glorified the gangster at the centre of the narrative. I think that the director was wrong to try and make us feel sorry for this cold-blooded killer.'

Identify what types of reading excerpts 1, 2 and 3 are giving.

Characters

Representations can be complex (Rainer Wenger in *The Wave)*, or more simplistic (Superman). In *The Wave*, Rainer Wenger is represented as a charismatic teacher, yet our sympathy towards him changes several times throughout the film and the ending can elicit many different spectator responses; likewise with David, the central character in *Tsotsi*. Our studies for Paper 1 and Paper 2 may have highlighted differences in terms of the 'ways in which specific characters or groups are represented. In the main, the central characters in the focus films for Paper 2 are more complex, more '**three-dimensional**', less stereotypical, than genre characters.

Genre films contain characters referred to as **generic types**. The Superhero genre typically features **stereotypical** and/or **archetypal** characters; for example, Lex Luther in *Superman* typifies the villain or evil genius. (For a further consideration of character types in the Superhero genre see Section 3.)

Social groups

Films can offer different representations of **gender**, **ethnicity**, **culture**, **social class** and age.

Gender

This term does NOT refer to being male or female. Rather it is about what a particular society or culture expects of a man or woman. It is important because it defines how an individual will fit into society. It therefore, links closely with culture and ethnicity.

Culture

Refers to our identity, how we perceive the world and ourselves within it. It is important because our culture shapes the way we think and act, it shapes our standards and behaviour. Communities achieve a sense of 'belonging' based upon sharing cultural beliefs and values (see more in Section 2.10 Ideology).

Persepolis and *Elektra*: two very different representations of gender and culture?

How are culture are gender represented in the stills shown here? What differences do you notice? Are there any similarities?

Rabbit-Proof Fence; 'See that bird? It is the Spirit bird. He will always look after you.'

Ethnicity

An important way in which people are identified is in terms of their ancestry. For example, where their parents or grandparents were born, and their shared social experience – food, religion, dress, physical appearance. It can also refer to a race, people or nation. *Bend it Like Beckham, Persepolis, Rabbit-Proof Fence and Yasmin* all deal with gender, culture and ethnicity. It's important to be aware that your own cultural beliefs and values affect the ways in which you respond to these representations, and to demonstrate your understanding of these complex terms.

Social class

Another difficult term! Traditionally, social class has referred to a group of people with similar levels of wealth, influence and status. Although there is considerable debate about the ways in which social class is defined, your class is typically defined by how much you earn, how much power you have, and how important you are (your status). The upper class is the smallest, richest class, then come the middle class, working class and, at the bottom of the ladder, is the 'lower class' – a term which usually refers to the poorest, most vulnerable members of society. *Ratcatcher* and *Tsotsi* are interesting films to look at in terms of social class.

Exam tip

When analysing the representation of social class it is useful to look at people and places. Ask how a particular character is represented – costume, dialogue, body language, props, and then consider what their environment (setting) adds to your response to that representation. Alternatively, you can examine how environment is represented and then analyse how that affects our 'reading' of a specific character.

Quickfire 13

How is social class represented in the still on the right?

Age

This is easy to define when looking at a single character. A little trickier when looking at an age group, especially if we use words such as young or old. Young could cover anyone from birth to 30 or even 40 (depending on who is talking). And old could encompass anyone from 30–100 plus, again depending on point-of-view. Try to be as specific as possible when talking about the representation of age within a film and to consider the film-maker's intentions. If a group of teenagers is shown, do they look and behave in a stereotypical way, or are they shown as individuals with complex personalities and motivations? Do their experiences change them? Do the group dynamics change and how is this shown?

Style

You should also consider style when examining representations. How techniques used by the film-maker (cinematography, sound, editing and mise-en-scène) combine to create particular kinds of representations. **Realism** is a difficult term to define but it basically involves the film-maker creating a narrative and setting that are believable. Both *Rabbit-Proof Fence* and *Persepolis* are based on true stories but these stories are presented in very different ways. Phillip Noyce, the director of *Rabbit-Proof Fence*, chose to use young Aboriginal, non-actors for his central characters and to set the film in the Australian Outback alongside the actual 1,000 mile fence that runs through its centre. Marjane Satrapi chose to animate her story. These choices made by the film-makers are important. **Social realism** (see next topic: Ideology) is often seen as a conscious attempt to resist stereotypical representations. It tries to do this by using a variety of techniques: non-actors, naturalistic lighting, and real locations, narratives which focus on social problems and so resist comforting resolutions.

Key terms

Realism
A believable representation of people, places and events.

Social realism
A style of film-making which deals with social issues and uses specific stylistic techniques.

Analyse the representation of setting and one particular character or social group in the opening sequence of your focus film for Paper 2 and a film you have studied for Paper 1. You should think about the following questions:

TASK 8

1. Who or what is being represented? Who is the preferred audience for this representation?

2. What is happening? Is the activity presented as typical, or atypical? Are they conforming to genre expectations or other conventions?

3. Where are they? How are they framed? Are they represented as natural or artificial? What surrounds them? What is in the foreground and what is in the background?

10: Ideology

Different ways of viewing the world

Ideology refers to the ways in which a particular culture, group, or individual, views the world – their **values** and **beliefs**. When studying ideology it is useful to consider:

- Who made the film and why?
- Which actors were used and why?
- Where was it made and why?

Who made it and why?

It's useful to consider where the ideas come from which led to the production of a film. Was it based on an existing novel, play or comic book? Who wrote the film script? Who directed the film? What have they done before? Can you spot any recurring ideas across a range of films involving these writers or directors? For example, Gavin Hood is a young South African director. He wrote the script for *Tsotsi* and also directed the film. Hood based the script on a short novel by Athol Fugard, one of South Africa's most famous playwrights. Fugard's novel dealt powerfully with themes such as poverty and inequality in apartheid South Africa. These ideas were clearly important for Hood. Below he outlines some of the values and beliefs he wanted to express in that movie:

'Tsotsi is a universal story not simply a South African story...It is essentially a story of a young person who struggles to find their identity without parental support or social support systems.'

Clearly then Hood's work contains a **political imperative**. At the beginning of the film Tsotsi is represented as a stereotypical young gangster but the binary oppositions of good vs evil don't work in this film, they are far too simplistic. He is a product of his environment and 'there but for fortune go you or I'. These values and beliefs also transfer to the films Hood has made in Hollywood. *Wolverine* is a very different in terms of genre and style but Hood's ideological viewpoint is still evident:

'Any movie that is simply about good versus evil...is in my view putting out into the world and certainly into a mass audience and young audience's mind a rather dangerous philosophy, which is that there is good and evil in the simplistic and easily defined way... '

Other films yield equally interesting views of the world. *Rabbit-Proof Fence* is a true story written by Doris Pilkington, the mother of Grace, the story's central character. Christine Olsen was so moved by Pilkington's story that she decided to adapt it for the screen. The film carries a universal message (as does *Tsotsi*) about racism and the need to respect other people's cultures.

Key terms

Values
Moral principles or standards.

Beliefs
Something that you accept as true.

Political imperative
Demanding a political solution to an urgent problem.

Exam tip

When asked about representation a high level response may also consider ideology. How the representation of particular themes and issues may convey important beliefs or values.

TASK 9

Research your focus film for Paper 2 – make notes on who made it and why, paying close attention to the ways in which the origin of stories, scriptwriters, director and producers affect the beliefs/values evidenced within the film.

Which actors were used and why?

If we think Hollywood, we automatically think big stars. Often these stars have come to signify particular values and beliefs. So, for example, we have come to associate Tobey Maguire with positive values. He is the clean-cut all-American young man who can be relied on to do the right thing. Perhaps this is why *Spiderman 3* irritated some fans. Spiderman was defying our expectations and so was Tobey Maguire!

Several of the films you have studied for Paper 2 deal with social and economic circumstances within particular groups in society. These include: poverty, crime and racism. Specific **social realist** techniques may be used in order to convey the importance of these social issues. These emphasise that the problems they deal with are 'real-life' problems and as such often don't have a resolution. One technique involves the use of non-actors usually alongside professional actors. Often the non-actors have experienced similar social problems to those affecting their film character. Directors hope that this experience will bring a greater degree of 'truth' or realism to their performances and perhaps even move the audience to help bring about change. *Ratcatcher*, *Rabbit-Proof Fence* and *Tsotsi* all feature non-actors. Often film producers make us aware of the non-actors' circumstances before making the film. This can affect our emotional response to that performance. For young people such as Presley Chweneyagae (Tsotsi) and Terry Pheto (Miriam) whose experiences of growing up in the townships just outside Johannesburg mirror those of the characters they play, beliefs and values can be seen to be played out in real life. Making *Tsotsi* has changed their lives, they have been given a chance to fulfil their potential but many, many more young people in South Africa and across the world will never be given that chance.

Name four other stars that have come to signify particular values or beliefs.

Rabbit-Proof Fence: The smiling Chief Protector decides which girl he can 'breed the blackness' out of

Where was it made and why?

Not all film-makers consciously make films that support or reflect the dominant ideologies within their countries. Often directors, producers and scriptwriters make films in countries that are not their own; for example, Guillermo Del Toro is Mexican, Gavin Hood is South African, Marjane Satrapi is Iranian. Thinking about why film-makers choose to make films elsewhere can also give you an insight into ideology. Satrapi had to make *Persepolis* outside her beloved Iran, her story revolves around the difficulties of living in Iran, especially for a woman. And yet, like Hood, she stresses that the beliefs and values that underpin her story and the issues dealt with are universal.

What might be the advantages and disadvantages of using non-actors in a film?

Persepolis: 'That was the last time I saw my grandmother – freedom always has a price'

43

However, many of the films you watch are strongly connected to the culture, values and beliefs of the country in which they were made. *The Wave*, for example, made in Germany, deals with the German past, present and future. Near the start of the film a student tells his teacher Rainer Wenger, that Germany would never tolerate another autocracy (referring to the rise of Fascism and Adolf Hitler). Yet Wenger's project highlights the dangers of becoming too complacent about the past.

The Wave: Karo explains that 'Autocracy is when an individual or group rules the masses'

In terms of *Tsotsi*, again the history of the country is vitally important. South Africa has an unjust, violent and troubled history. Apartheid (a racist system of government in which the majority black South Africans were ruled by a white minority) collapsed in the 1990s. However, a huge majority of South Africans still live in poverty. This poverty also brings with it associated problems of crime, drug addiction and disease. *Tsotsi* highlights the need to address these problems urgently especially if the younger generation are going to be given hope for the future.

Your studies for Paper 1 and Paper 2 will have highlighted that different countries may use different cinematic styles, representations or narrative structures. These similarities and differences may reflect beliefs, values and ideas. There is often a strong relationship between ideology and genre, for example the Superhero genre. If you study the still below of Captain America, aspects of America's dominant ideologies are clearly signalled.

● What's in a name? – Well Captain America covers: high ranking, commanding, strong, fighting for 'right', protecting others. What's in the costume? Army uniform, leather 'bomber' jacket making him look even larger, more muscular, again emphasising strength.

● Who is he 'shielding'? – Himself! The stars and stripes protect him from evil cowards who are more than likely to 'stab him in the back' both literally and metaphorically. As long as he wears it and stays true to all it symbolises he will be safe.

● Who is he shielding? – Us! As long as we pledge our allegiance to the ultimate Captain

America (the American State) we will be safe, and that's not just Americans but every other country in the world.

The beliefs and values that typically drive the Superhero movie revolve around American supremacy and its role in protecting everybody else in the world. So Superheroes don't just save America they save the world and protect the 'American values' of freedom, democracy, life, liberty and the pursuit of happiness (as defined by Americans).

11: Conclusion

Hopefully this 'micro' and macro' film section will have underlined the importance of understanding what we mean by the term 'film language'. Your knowledge and understanding of this key area will provide you with a strong foundation for both examined papers and your controlled assessment work. Although we have looked at each element separately, by now you should be aware that all of the parts work together to create meaning. So when you are asked a question about any of the 'macro' elements, representation, narrative, or genre, you must consider the role of 'micro' elements in your analysis. Use your 'terminology tool kits' when revising, they will provide you with the appropriate language to consider how meaning and response are created at the highest level.

Finally, as a member of an audience you will have a personal response to a film you have watched. In terms of personal response there are no right or wrong answers so just let 'your mind take a walk'. Describe what you see on the screen in detail, talk about the various techniques used and then take time to explore how it has made you feel. So, for example, if the end of *Tsotsi* makes you cry (it does me and I've seen it over a dozen times) don't be afraid to say so. Take a few moments though to think how this emotion has been elicited. Is it performance working in tandem with cinematography? Tsotsi's facial expressions showing his feelings of vulnerability, bewilderment, loss and fear shown through repeated close-ups which communicate to you more powerfully than words could ever do? Or is it that your initial sense of relief when he is not killed is quickly supplanted by the realisation that this film has no happy resolution and the future for Tsotsi is most certainly prison? Whatever your personal response, just make sure you express it clearly and analyse why you've responded in a particular way.

Quickfire answers:

1a. A medium or mid shot

1b. The teacher (Rainer Wenger) is placed firmly centre frame. His arms are outstretched so he almost fills the whole of the frame. The blackboard at the back of him is also in sharp focus and we can clearly read the word 'Autokratie' (autocracy), in fact it almost seems to be coming out of his head like a speech bubble. The students are pushed to the sides and are partly excluded from the frame, Wenger's arms almost seem to be creating that push.

1c. Autocracy means dictatorship, or absolute rule by one person. This is an important, powerful character, he looks straight at the camera, and our eyes are drawn to him. Clearly, the framing is forcing us to make the link between this character and the idea of dictatorship.

2a. This shot highlights the importance of this character and his emotions. At this point in the action Marco finally confronts Wenger about the terrible consequences of his project and his teaching methods. This is the moment in the film when Marco takes centre stage. The audience needs to understand his emotions; his expression conveys a mixture of determination and fear as he looks over his shoulder at Wenger behind him on the stage.

2b. This shot shows very little background, and concentrates on either a face, or a specific detail of mise-en-scène. Everything else is just a blur in the background, so the importance of this character and his emotions is emphasised. The other students in the background are out of focus, we do not know at this point what their reaction to Marco's defiance will be.

3. Superhero movies are typically set in a big **Metropolis** usually New York or somewhere that looks very like it. These cities are usually modern with lots of modern, high rise buildings. Often 'iconic' buildings/structures are featured such as the Statue of Liberty or The White House.

4a. Low angle, long shot.

4b. It makes the Sandman look even larger and more threatening, brings him closer to the audience creating more tension/excitement.

5a. Child's eye-level shot positioned lower than the typical 5–6 feet from ground level used for an adult's eye-level shot.

5b. A low angle shot making the creature appear even larger and more threatening.

5c. A high angle shot emphasising the height of the building and showing how far the woman has to fall.

5d. A bird's-eye view shot looking directly down over the city.

5e. An oblique or canted shot, suggesting Batman's drugged state.

6. Top lighting which 'floods' the ground where Pepper Potts is standing. The back lighting appears to come from the wall light just above her head. This creates a halo effect. The top lighting suggests that there is something above her head casting a strong light. This emphasises her body language. Her open mouth, upward gaze with eyes wide-open, suggests that what she is looking at is large and awe-inspiring. She is centre frame and obviously vulnerable.

7. Low key lighting with secondary back light (appearing to come from window).

8. There is a lot you can say about this still. The dark, hidden location suggests it may contain hidden secrets. The vaulted roof and cavernous space make Carlos seem very small. His vulnerability is emphasised by his pyjamas and bare feet. Although in the foreground the young character appears dwarfed by the dark stone walls – a back light casts his shadow in front of him. He is moving toward the source of the light and the pool. We can't see the expression on his face but he is neither running away, nor obviously scared.

9. In terms of your interpretation of mise-en-scène, there are no absolute right or wrong answers to this question! If you were studying this film you would perhaps realise that the window represents the kind of world that James would love and it's a sharp contrast to the poverty of environment that his own home represents.

10. *Spiderman* is a good example. Peter Parker is the

typical American High School 'nerd'. He is keen on Science and is bullied by the school 'jocks'. He struggles to keep a job, or get a girl. His clothes and personality underline just how easily ignored and insignificant he is. Spiderman, on the other hand, is a heroic figure, admired by the public and adored by women. His superpowers, costume and personality make him stand out from the crowd; there is no way he can be ignored!

11. 1 = preferred reading, 2 = negotiated reading, 3 = oppositional reading.

12. Both stills feature women. The first shows a group of girls in a classroom. We know their religion because it is signalled by their hijabs (traditional Muslim dress). They all look almost identical, we cannot see their figures or their hair, the fact that this is an animation adds to this feeling of a common identity. However, if we look more closely, we can learn things about particular characters. The girl in the middle appears to be making a speech and the others are smiling and applauding. She may look almost identical but she is centre frame. One girl has her hand over her mouth signalling a slight shock at what is being said. These girls may come from a culture where women are expected to cover their bodies and act modestly but overall a feeling of solidarity and strength is communicated.

The second still is much more 'realistic' in terms of style, and yet both females adopt almost identical poses, identical hairstyles and facial expressions. The figure at the front of the frame is bigger and clearly older; her costume is low cut and tight fitting accentuating her curves. The two women are clearly more sexualised in terms of representation but a sense of kinship, strength and solidarity is also signalled.

13. It underlines the poverty and hardships of the people living in South Africa's townships. There is a terrible storm, it is late at night and yet people are still queuing at the well in order to pump their water. They wait patiently to fill their buckets, people are still selling stores by the wayside, and a man is wheeling a barrow with what looks like grain in. Obviously life is so hard the inhabitants of the township have to work long hours in order to scrape a living. The township has the appearance of a scrapheap. Dwellings are ramshackle, made from, things that have been discarded by others – inhabitants are disregarded, consigned to the scrapheap by other wealthier classes.

14. Take your pick! Jack Nicholson – the villain with a charming side, not fully responsible for his bad behaviour. Chris Reeves – strong, upholder of American values even in the light of almost insurmountable odds. Audrey Tatou – a particular mixture of innocence and charm, beautiful and stylish, quintessentially 'French'.

15. The advantages revolve around the 'truth' of a particular performance. So, for example, Presley Chweneyagae (Tsotsi) and Terry Pheto (Miriam), who grew up in the townships outside Johannesburg, were able to bring a 'naturalness' and real insight into life there through their performances. The disadvantages lie in their lack of training in terms of performance, learning lines and knowing what is expected on set. They also do not have the international selling power that big Hollywood stars bring to the films they act in.

Section 3: Paper 1 – The Superhero Genre

1: Introduction

Your first examination contains four compulsory questions focusing on the Superhero genre. These questions assess your knowledge and understanding of film language and key industry and audience issues. This part of the book is designed to cover all of the areas you will need to revise in preparation for the exam. It has been organised into five major sections. The first three sections address three key questions designed to consolidate your understanding of the strong relationship between the Hollywood film industry and the concept of genre – in this case specifically the Superhero genre:

- What is Hollywood?
- What is a Superhero?
- What is a Superhero movie?

The fourth section looks in depth at what we mean by the term genre, focusing upon codes and conventions. You will need to have a clear understanding of these in order to tackle each of the four examination questions.

The fifth industry section covers the ways in which Superhero movies are marketed; your knowledge and understanding of this area is assessed in Questions 3 and 4 on Paper 1.

Finally, just in case you are anxious about exam skills, or are concerned about your approach to specific questions, the last section takes you through the examination and suggests strategies that will help you to feel more confident. Just bear in mind though that there are no 'quick fixes' in terms of exam preparation, and carefully planned revision and hard work are invariably the key to exam success.

Key term

Revenue or box office
The money a film generates in ticket sales. A reference to where people traditionally buy their tickets.

2: The Hollywood film industry

What is Hollywood?

Paper 1 is all about looking in more depth at those films, and the industry that produces them. This largely means the American film industry, or Hollywood as it is more commonly referred to. In 2012 Hollywood's total reported **revenue** was $10.71 billion, this focus on finance influences the films we see for good and bad. Hollywood pursues financial success and this is a big reason why it likes genre so much. When it finds a genre that the cinema-going audience likes then it will concentrate on this whilst it remains successful. One of the most successful genres of recent times has been the Superhero movie and this is why it is the focus of Paper 1.

How profitable are May's big blockbuster films?

TASK 1

The worldwide marketing budgets for Hollywood films are huge but so are the profits made. Below are the budgets for some of May 2013's biggest releases:

	Budget/marketing	Projected global gross profit
Iron Man 3 (Disney/ Marvel)	$ 375 million	$ 1.28 billion
The Great Gatsby (Village Roadshow)	$ 280 million	$ 345 million
Star Trek Into Darkness (Par/Skydance)	$ 365 million	$ 490 million
Hangover Part 3 (Warners Legendary)	$ 253 million	$ 375 million
Fast & Furious 6 (Universal)	$ 335 million	$ 730 million

1. How many of these have you seen?
2. What are the popular genres?
3. Which seems to be the most popular genre?
4. Can you think of any reasons why?

Why is Hollywood so dominant?

Many people don't even realise that the bulk of films in our cinemas come from just one industry. This dominance takes many forms, the sheer number of films shown in **mainstream cinemas**, their overwhelming presence in advertising, film magazines and most other media outlets. This dominance comes from their focus on financial success which gives them the power to dominate. It comes initially from the size of their own film market which is ten times the size of Britain's, with such an advantage it is no real surprise it is difficult to compete with them. The factor of ten pops up in many areas, they have ten times more cinema screens, budgets tend to be up to ten times higher. So when we look at a popular **blockbuster** genre like Superheroes it's not unusual to find very few non-American examples. *Kick-Ass*, despite appearance, was a British-based Superhero movie with a $30m **budget** (an even lower $28m for *Kick-Ass 2*), *Iron Man 2* the same year had a $200m budget – over six times higher. So it is not difficult to see how this financial 'clout' gives Hollywood such an advantage and why keeping and using the blockbuster movie is such an important strategy for them.

How is Hollywood organised?

Hollywood is not just one single entity. The American film industry is made up of **studios**, those familiar names we see at the start of most films. The main ones are Disney, Warner Brothers, Paramount, Universal, 20th Century Fox and Sony (Columbia). These all have control over **production** and **distribution**, two of the three stages of the film industry, the third being **exhibition** which they use the power of their films' popularity to heavily influence as well. Most have at least one Superhero franchise:

Studio	Property /Franchise
Disney	Marvel: *Iron Man, Captain America, Thor, The Avengers*
Warner Bros.	DC: *Batman, Superman, Green Lantern*
Universal	*Hulk* (now back with Marvel), *Kick-Ass*
20th Century Fox	*Fantastic Four, X-Men, Wolverine*
Paramount	Sold their final Marvel distribution rights to Disney in 2013
Sony	*Spiderman, Ghost Rider, Hancock*

So as we can see that for at least four of the big six studios Superhero movies are important '**tent pole**' franchises, even without Superhero movies Universal still has successes like *The Fast and the Furious* and Paramount have *Star Trek* and the *Transformers* to generate big **box office** returns.

It is not just about making films with massive budgets, at least $200m for a blockbuster these days, it is also about the power to sell them once they have been made. If there is one area where Hollywood truly excels, it is their willingness to spend money in persuading us to go and see them. Marvel's *The Avengers* cost $220m to make and it is estimated that they spent nearly as much (if not more) on marketing it. How this money is spent and how it is supposed to generate ticket sales is an important element of what we study for Paper 1.

Key terms

Mainstream cinemas
Cinemas (typically multiplex) that are often part of a cinema chain and predominantly feature big budget American productions.

Blockbuster
A big budget film that takes over $100 million at the US box office.

Budget
The amount of money spent on either making the movie or marketing the movie or both.

Studios
Organisations that arrange funding to make and distribute films.

Production
Activities involved in the actual making of the film.

Distribution
Deciding where a film will be shown and publicising this.

Exhibition
Where the film is shown – cinemas of varying types.

Property
Any source of ideas that has been used to create a film.

Franchise
Where a film and its often planned sequels are part of a larger business entity.

'Tent pole' film
A film, the success of which, will 'hold up' or support the studio's other projects.

Below is a list of 2012's most profitable films:

	Film	Domestic	International	Worldwide
1	**The Avengers** Disney/Marvel	$623.4 M	$888.4 M	$1.51 B
2	**The Dark Knight Rises** Warner Bros.	$448.1 M	$632.9 M	$1.08 B
3	**Skyfall** Sony/MGM	$289.6 M	$710.6 M	$1.00 B
4	**Ice Age: Continental Drift** 20th Century Fox	$161.1 M	$714.0 M	$875.1 M
5	**Twilight Saga: Breaking Dawn 2** Summit	$286.1 M	$520.0 M	$806.1 M
6	**The Amazing Spider-Man** Sony	$262.0 M	$490.2 M	$752.2 M
7	**Madagascar 3** Paramount/Dreamworks Animation	$261.4 M	$525.7 M	$742.1 M
8	**The Hobbit: An Unexpected Journey** Warner Bros./New Line/MGM	$221.4 M	$464.0 M	$685.4 M
9	**The Hunger Games** Lionsgate	$408.0 M	$278.5 M	$686.5 M
10	**Men in Black 3** Sony	$179.0 M	$445.0 M	$624.0 M
11	**Brave** Disney/Pixar	$237.2 M	$298.1 M	$535.3 M

1. Which genres are popular?

2. Which seems to be the most popular single genre?

3. Which is the most popular market? (Domestic refers to the USA.)

4. Are blockbuster movies still popular?

TaSK 2

The future?

Recent debate has been on whether the blockbuster strategy is still successful. This has led to the studios making fewer films overall, particularly those with less marketable subjects, and more modest budgets. Recent disappointments for the studios include *John Carter*, *The Lone Ranger*, *R.I.P.D.*, *Jack The Giant Slayer*, *Turbo*, *Pacific Rim* and *After Earth*. Many people (including Steven Spielberg) have questioned whether this approach can continue.

With an overall US box office of $4.1bn close to 2011's record of $4.4bn then the debate remains open. Blockbusters, Superhero or otherwise, seem set to remain for the foreseeable future.

Hollywood never stands still when it comes to new business. China is seen as potentially the biggest film market in the world and many blockbusters have been tailored for the market, even shooting scenes exclusive to the Chinese-released *Iron Man 3* among them.

Quickfire

1

Why are blockbusters so important to Hollywood?

3: What is a Superhero?

The key to defining the Superhero movie is to have a firm grasp on what we mean by a Superhero. It is not as simple as somebody with superpowers because not all of them have superpowers. Our definition may look something like this:

A Superhero can be defined as an individual who uses their power(s) for public rather than personal good, often against an enemy who uses their powers for personal rather than public good. 'Powers' are defined as qualities (or resources) that go far beyond the limitations of normal people.

This definition includes the obvious candidates such as Superman and Spiderman alongside Batman and Iron Man whose great wealth and intelligence/training allow them to act as other 'super-powered' heroes do.

Where do Superheroes come from?

Most can be found initially in **comic books**. This is important for the studios as it means they have established characters and histories (often referred to as **canon**). So there is already a fan base built in and in many cases a recognition factor that makes their marketing easier. This is why popular properties, for example the Harry Potter books, or Superman comics, attract studio funding. Studios are willing to pay a big premium when it comes to buying the right to make movies, this popularity is seen as one way to reduce the risk of failure at the box office.

Although there are many Superheroes and movies not based on Marvel and DC comics, these are by far the most important sources for Superhero movies.

DC (Detective Comics)

Owned by Warner Brothers studios. It was founded in 1934 and is the older of the two major comic book publishers. Golden age heroes such as Batman (Bob Kane and Bill Finger) first appeared in 1938 with Superman (Jerry Siegel and Joe Shuster)

DC: Superman and friends

following in 1939. Many more Superheroes and villains came after, including Wonder Woman, The Flash, Green Lantern, Captain Marvel, Hawkman, The Teen Titans, Green Arrow, Aquaman, Robin, Supergirl, Batgirl, The Justice League, Lex Luthor, The Joker, The Riddler, and Catwoman.

Marvel

Marvel was founded as Timely Comics just a few years after DC in 1939. It was re-named Marvel Comics in the early 1960s. Marvel's golden age heroes included Prince Namor and The Human Torch from the 1930s with Captain America arriving as a patriotic symbol in the 1940s. In the 1960s Stan Lee along with artists Jack Kirby and Steve Ditko and others created the now familiar Spiderman, Hulk, X-Men, Fantastic Four, Thor, Iron Man, The Avengers and many others.

Marvel: Spiderman and friends

The independents

Independent comic book publishers are typically much smaller than the big two and quite often deal with subjects and characters outside of the mainstream of Superheroes. Dark Horse Comics gave us – *Hellboy* (2004), *Sin City* (2005), *The Mask* (1994), *The Mystery Men* (1999) spoof and the quasi-Superheroic *300* (2006). Picked up and distributed by Marvel (comic) and Lionsgate and Universal (film), British film gave us *Kick-Ass* (2010). If we add to this **original screenplays** such as *Unbreakable* (2000), *The Incredibles* (2004) and *Hancock* (2008) we can begin to see that the Superhero movie is far from the exclusive province of DC and Marvel Comics.

Conclusion

Hopefully, you now have a clear idea of what a Superhero is and where they come from. We should remember that the Superhero movie was born elsewhere, in the comic book. This has the advantage of providing an established fan base plus a rich heritage of characters and stories to draw from, but this can also be a drawback when it comes to being taken seriously.

Key term

Original screenplay
A script for a film based on a 'new' idea and not an existing property.

Why is the comic book history of the character important to film?

4: What is a Superhero movie?

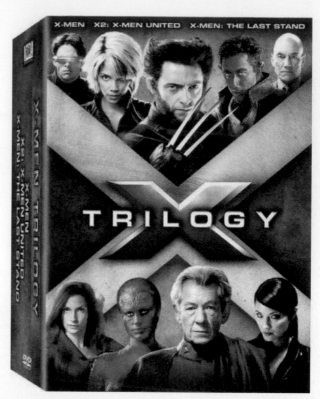

Typical characters?

Key terms

Stereotype
A simplistic way of representing people, places or social groups.

Archetype
An instantly recognisable representation of a character that has been in use for a very long time.

Exam tip

Apply these codes and conventions to as many films as you can. Try to build up a list of the most typical things in Superhero movies.

Exam tip

Have a good range of examples to use in your exam.

To answer this question we have to consider the 'rules' – those things that we use to define any genre, its codes and conventions:

1. Setting – its location or historical time period.

2. Themes – ideas, concepts and/or emotions it deals with.

3. Characters – powers, secret identity, **stereotypes** and **archetypes**.

4. Props or significant objects – the small things or details we expect.

5. Narrative and plot – typical kinds of stories that are told.

6. Style – use of film language, the look of the film, editing, shots, cinematography.

For a film to be considered as part of the Superhero genre it must share some, or all, of the codes and conventions used in other 'Superhero' films. They don't have to be exactly the same, there will be both differences and similarities, but they should have enough points of similarity for us to be able to say 'yes that's a close enough fit, we can call it a Superhero movie'.

Here are a few basics with examples from *X-Men* (2000). You should use your own studies and knowledge to refine these examples:

● Props or significant objects: a costume and/or gadgets are often used as a '**McGuffin**' to drive the narrative, for example the X-Men costumes, Magneto's helmet, Cerebro, Magneto's power-transferring machine.

● Setting: typically a contemporary often un-named American city, e.g. New York.

● Themes: these can be divided into 'the public', the visible struggles of the hero, and 'the private', the personal struggles of the hero. For example, the public's fear of people who are different, or those we don't understand. The private, Rogue's relationship problems, Wolverine's search for his past.

- Characters: the characters we typically expect. For example, Professor X and the X-Men, Magneto and The Brotherhood of Evil Mutants. These are **binary opposites**.

- Narrative and plot: good vs evil and sometimes an origin story, e.g. helping humanity vs subduing them. The origin of mutation and the powers it confers.

- Style: action – fights and destruction, CGI, e.g. Wolverine vs Sabretooth, realistic depiction and cinematography to increase believability. CGI providing spectacle, showing the various powers and abilities.

So, although we knew before we started that *X-Men* was a Superhero movie, the important thing is that we have used the codes and conventions to gather evidence to prove it. We will look at each of these codes and conventions in more detail in the forthcoming topics.

Why is genre so important?

There are two ways of looking at this, from the point of view of the audience and from the point of view of the industry:

- Audience: enables us to identify films we enjoy and to understand the films.

- Industry: helps them identify films people want to see and can be used as a kind of 'formula' for producing them.

Conclusion

Remember most Superhero films will readily fit the codes and conventions, we just have to think carefully as to where to find the evidence. Those that are more interesting are films that don't quite fit all the categories so we have to decide and argue for ourselves whether they fit or not.

Key terms

McGuffin
An object the securing of which sometimes drives the narrative forward.
'The object around which the plot revolves, but, as to what that object *specifically* is', he declared, 'the audience don't care'.
Alfred Hitchcock

Binary opposites
Characters that represent sets of opposite values, e.g. good and evil, light and dark.

What are other popular genres and why?

Wolverine – typical costume and weapons?

5: Genre codes and conventions

Location

Typically this is an **urban** setting. This affords the hero plenty of crime-fighting opportunities and when the super-villain comes along it maximises the opportunities for large-scale **jeopardy** and destruction. This is an often non-specific un-named American city. However, in the Marvel universe it tends to be New York as that is where many of the heroes are based. *Iron Man* and Tony Stark being a partial exception as his playboy lifestyle has drawn him from New York to the west coast and Los Angeles. In the DC universe it can be different fictional versions of New York, the dark and gritty one of Gotham, and the more conventional metropolitan version of **Metropolis** in *Superman*. Most Superheroes at least start to ply their trade on the seamier side of urban America where their main protagonist (the criminal) can be found; it is about dark alleys and dangerous places, Superheroes sometimes protecting specific neighbourhoods.

Additionally a Superhero's job will often involve saving the world, so locations often go global, *The Fantastic Four* (2005), or even intergalactic, *The Green Lantern* (2011).

It will also involve headquarters both secret (*X-Men*'s Xavier's school for the gifted), and public (*The Fantastic Four*'s Baxter Building). The more famous secret headquarters perhaps belonging to DC in the form of *Batman*'s 'Batcave' and *Superman*'s 'Fortress Of Solitude'.

Exam tip

Always try to discuss the use of the setting rather than just describing it.

Exam tip

Revise both typical and non-typical examples.

A typical urban setting, in this case New York

Stark Tower prominent on the New York skyline

Time period

The time period is almost exclusively contemporary except for when an origin story looks back over a longer period of time, e.g. *Captain America* in the 1940s. The future can sometimes put in an appearance particularly if it's in jeopardy as in the forthcoming *X-Men Days Of Future Past* film.

Conclusion

Remember when dealing with setting to consider the following questions:

● Is it a typical (one you would expect) location?

● What makes it typical or untypical?

● Why has that location been chosen?

● What visual impact does it have?

● What is its narrative importance?

● How is it being used by the film-maker?

Quickfire 4

Name some of the films that don't use New York. What might the reasons be for this?

6: Props and significant objects

The Superhero movie is rich in the kind of details we expect in the broad category of props and significant objects.

Costume

Would a Superhero be a Superhero without a costume? Here are some of the functions it serves:

● It preserves their secret identity, helps to identify them as a hero (or villain).

● It provides a powerful marketing tool to sell the character and film. Instantly recognisable examples are Spiderman's and Superman's red and blue costumes.

However, Superhero costumes can work in different ways. Spiderman's costume definitely acts to keep Peter Parker's true identity a secret. Whereas Superman's is all about drawing attention to the hero, Clark Kent is the disguise. Symbolism is also important; often costumes speak to ideology and patriotism. For example, the red, white and blue of Captain America and Superman and the American flag. The American flag is a symbol of American values. The Superhero wearing the colours and the stars and the stripes of the American flag also champions these values: freedom, equality, democracy, champion of the little guy, helper of the oppressed and defender against tyranny!

The American flag goes to war, unmistakable symbolism in the costume

Gadgets, weapons and tools

These can be used to enhance, or act, instead of superpowers.

Batman is perhaps the most famous on the 'gadget front' with his utility belt and all the weapons and crime-fighting tools it contains.

Costumes often differ from their comic book versions, why might this be?

Batman's 'utility belt

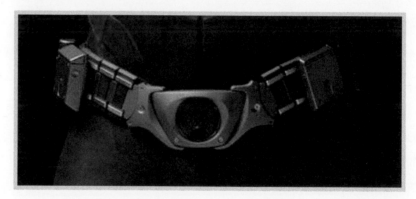

Thor's magic hammer Mjolnir is both a powerful weapon and a symbol of his worth and power as a god and prince of Asgard. Captain America uses his vibranium shield skillfully both as a defensive prop and a weapon.

Two props clash and two props team up *Avengers Assemble* (2012)

Vehicles

These are often iconic parts of the Superhero's identity.

Batman has the Batmobile, perhaps the most famous Superhero vehicle.

The X-Men have their Blackbird jet.

The Fantastic Four the Fantasticar.

The Avengers and Shield have the vehicle/headquarters in the form of the Helicarrier.

Batmobile from *Batman* (1989) and *Batman Returns* (1992)

The Blackbird jet

The Fantastic Four's Fantasticar

The Helicarrier

Exam tip

Consider both the practical as well as symbolic importance of props.

Exam tip

Revise both typical and non-typical examples.

Props or significant objects are important typical 'ingredients' in the Superhero genre. They serve a number of functions. Firstly they provide excitement and/or spectacle for the audience. They create opportunities for Superheroes such as Ironman or Batman, who have not been born with special powers, to wage the battle of good versus evil effectively.

'McGuffins'

Props and significant objects can also serve an important narrative function. A McGuffin is a narrative device which features some goal, desired object, or other motivator, that the protagonist pursues. Often there is little or no explanation as to why it is considered so important. The most common type of McGuffin is an object, place or person. McGuffins are important in Superhero narratives where typically the hero and villain fight to gain control over objects which enable them access to money, power, strength or love. In *Thor* (2011) the Casket of Ancient Winters is a big threat as it is the Frost Giants' source of power. In both *Captain America* (2011) and *Avengers Assemble* (2012) the Tesseract is a vital part of both The Red Skull's and Loki's plans.

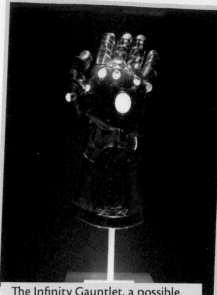

The Infinity Gauntlet, a possible future Marvel McGuffin?

Task 3

- Download two still images from your computer – one hero and one villain. Annotate the images in order to highlight the importance of props and costume for each character.

- Find an example of a McGuffin in a Superhero film you have studied. Write a short paragraph explaining its importance in narrative function.

7: Style

Exam tip

Style can often be a difficult aspect to discuss. Concentrate on specific examples that are common to more than one film.

The style of a genre is about the overall look and feel of the films. This includes how film language is typically used and the kind of shots and sequences we expect to see. The typical uses of camera, sound, editing and mise-en-scène in Superhero movies, in many aspects of style, conform to what we would expect from an action movie. A quick overall pace, with some slower moments to provide contrast or 'shade' for explosive action sequences.

Exam tip

Revise examples of style that can both compare and contrast with each other.

A different approach to hijacking in *The Dark Knight Rises* (2012) – big action set pieces are an important feature of Superhero movie style

However, the Superhero movie differs from the action film because its original source material is more visual than most others, the comic book being a storyboard of sorts. So we will often see elements of comic book presentation being used in the film. Whole **panels** (single comic book pictures) are sometimes transplanted to the screen. For example, when Peter Parker throws away his costume in *Spiderman 2* (2004) the scene is almost identical to a classic comic book cover depicting the same 'Spiderman no more' storyline. Other Superhero films have incorporated even more comic book features into their style. One example would be *Hulk* (2003) which used **split-screen** techniques to imitate the panel structure of a comic book. *Kick-Ass* (2010) used elements of comic book style throughout. Screen captions were styled like the lettering of a comic book, and comic book art was used to tell the **back story** of Nicolas Cage's Big Daddy character.

When thinking about the style of Superhero movies it is important to compare and contrast different films so you can get a feel for the typical uses of film language. The more films you watch the better 'feel' for this style you will have.

Key terms

Panel
A single frame or picture in a comic book.

Split-screen
When a film is edited with more than one sequence happening simultaneously on screen.

Back story
The history of a character that has happened prior to the events in the film's narrative.

Big Daddy's back story told in animated comic book form in *Kick-Ass* (2010)

Quickfire
6

What are the major differences in terms of style between an Action movie and a Superhero movie?

8: Characters

In thinking about the characters seen in Superhero movies we again need to look at those that are typical of the genre. Most of them can be found on this list:

- **Hero**: The straightforward hero, initially reluctant at times, usually male. The one with the superpowers or their equivalent.

- **Villain**: The main opposition to the hero. They will have their own superpower that they use to further their 'evil schemes'.

- **The 'side swapper'**: The hero turned villain / the villain turned hero, super-villains can be someone who tried being a hero and changed sides.

- **Bad guys**: The lower rank of criminal that the hero tests themself against; common thieves, muggers, bank robbers and so on.

Exam tip

Always try to discuss both what is generic and unique about the characters you choose.

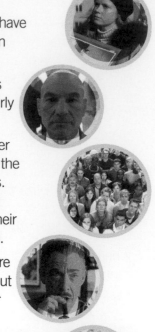

Key Term

Vox pop
Comes from the Latin phrase *vox populi,* meaning 'voice of the people'. It most commonly refers to the kind of random interview conducted in the street.

- **The strong woman**: They are usually a 'career girl' type and have been an ever present since Lois Lane appeared in Superman way back in 1978.

- **The mentor**: A Superhero will often have somebody he turns to for guidance or inspiration who acts as a mentor, particularly during their development or in times of doubt and difficulty.

- **The public**: Whilst not strictly speaking an individual character in their own right, they do perform several important roles in the different guises they appear in throughout Superhero movies. As individuals they provide the victims for the hero to protect and rescue and will often be interviewed '**vox pop**' style for their opinions as to whether the hero is a force for good or for bad.

- **Authority figures**: These are often representations of the more conventional controlling side of society. Whilst not being an out and out enemy of the hero they will often persecute them for their own reasons.

- **Supporters**: Closely related to the mentor are the Superhero's supporters. These are the people that have an important role in the hero's mission; again sometimes they will share the hero's true identity sometimes not.

Exam tip

Study similar and different characters from a range of Superhero films.

Task 4

Make a table similar to the one begun below which lists character types, their narrative function and gives an example from some of the films you have studied.

Character	Function	Examples
Hero	The character who has to save the world when it is threatened by the 'forces of evil'. Often has special powers which they use for good.	Superman Spiderman
Villain	The bad character who threatens the hero and the wider population. Can have special powers which are used for evil.	Green Goblin Magneto

Quickfire 7

Which character best represents what it means to be a Superhero?

Conclusion

In discussing these characters we can find some of the macro theory useful and should consider stereotypes, archetypes and representation.

We should also remember the marketing aspect of the main characters in particular. The Superhero is usually the star rather than the actor playing them, which is the usual marketing ploy. So it is Spiderman or Batman that helps sell the movie rather than the actor who plays them.

9: Narratives

The types of stories we come to expect in a particular category of films are known as genre narratives. When studying the Superhero movie it is important to focus upon typical narratives – the stories we might expect when going to see this kind of movie.

Typically a new Superhero **franchise** starts with an **origin story** before going on to develop other adventures for the character or characters. In the case of the Marvel cinematic universe this is more complicated as parts of one film's narrative often play a (small) part in another.

The narrative (the story of a film and how it is constructed) and plot (the more detailed plan of how the story is to be told) of Superhero movies is often described as **formulaic**. To some this means that many Superhero movies are the same film with a new 'cape' and a different cast. This may be true, to some extent, as most have a **linear narrative** (rather than **episodic** or **cyclical**) which leads to a final confrontation with the villain. As with most clearly genre films what counts is how the film-makers use this formula to entertain the audience.

A criticism of the genre is that the audience knows that the Superhero won't die and this renders any jeopardy they are placed in unconvincing. However, we may know this is a character decades old, that has never died (they are sometimes beaten), but the character(s) do not know this so we can still share **vicariously** in their jeopardy.

Other narrative ideas

In terms of narrative viewpoint the Superhero movie typically has the audience share the point of view of the hero, but not entirely. This is a mix of both **omniscient** and **restrictive** viewpoints (see Section 2.8: Narrative). We know more than most of the 'average' characters in the film, but there are often things we don't know because the hero does not know them either. Sometimes we are aware of a threat when they are not. This mix is used to engage us and involve us in different kinds of jeopardy as the film progresses, we fear with and for the hero.

Other narrative techniques can also be found from time to time such as **flashback** and **parallel narratives**. In *The Fantastic Four* (2005) we get occasional flashbacks to the time before they became Superheroes. For a while Doom's story runs parallel to theirs as he is drawn to villainy and they are drawn to good.

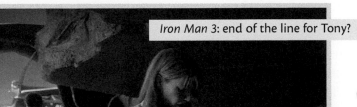

Iron Man 3: end of the line for Tony?

QUICKFIRE

8

Can you think any Superhero movie that has a cyclical narrative?

Key terms

Franchise
Where a film and its often planned sequels are part of a larger business entity.

Origin story
A narrative that explains how a character came by their powers and became a Superhero.

Formulaic
Where a film contains the same ingredients as others.

Linear narrative
A story that starts at the beginning and works to the end chronologically.

Episodic narrative
A story divided into separate episodes usually based around different characters.

Cyclical narrative
A story that starts at the end and works backwards.

Vicariously
To experience something indirectly or via a substitute.

Omniscient narrative
A narrative which allows us to know more about the characters and their situations than they know themselves.

Restricted narrative
A narrative that only allows us to know what the characters know.

Flashback
Where a character remembers past events in order to show the audience what happened.

Parallel narratives
When two or more characters share different stories that centre on the same event.

Exam tip
Always try to figure out what structure the film has to use in any answers.

Exam tip
Try to have an example of each of the different narratives and their features.

TASK 5

- Briefly outline the story of two of your study films.
- Explore the differences and similarities in terms of narrative between both films.

10: Themes and ideas

When we consider themes and ideas it is important to think about typicality. To ask 'What are the recurring themes and ideas that are evidenced across a range of Superhero movies?'. These themes tend to split into those centred on the 'private' or the individual, and those centred on the 'public' or 'bigger picture'.

'With great power comes great responsibility.' *Spiderman 2002*

The private – or individual themes

Motivation. Many of the individual themes are raised by the central question of 'Why do they do what they do?'

Revenge. One of the most common motivations for the hero's fight against crime is that of revenge. The desire to avenge the death of loved-ones is often the first step on the road to a wider mission.

Self-preservation and self-sacrifice. Sometimes the hero will have to give up, for example, a normal life to follow their calling, or indeed make sure they are seen to be acting for good to make sure that the public don't turn on them.

Redemption. Making good for previous wrongs is a theme most associated with evil in the Superhero movie and it crosses the divide between hero and villain with both often acting to redeem their past actions.

Relationships. These are a vital component in the Superhero movie in extending it beyond the confines of the 'big bang' special effect. As in any film all kinds of relationships feature – friendship, enmity, love, in fact any kind you can name.

The moral question. One theme that all Superheroes have to deal with is the moral question of the right and wrong of their actions and whether their transgression in the cause of good is right or wrong.

Exam tip

Remember that there may be multiple themes at play when you are asked to discuss a film.

TASK 6

Can you match one or more Superheroes to each individual theme?

Key terms

Motivation
The cause of an action of some kind.

Redemption
Improved or saved.

Moral
Sense of right or wrong.

Exam tip

Compile a list of the films you have seen and identify their themes.

Choices

Perhaps the choices heroes have to make are the most important 'private' themes of all. Heroes will inevitably be confronted with difficult choices as Spiderman's Uncle Ben says, 'With great power comes great responsibility'.

The 'public'

As with many films, Superhero movies touch on wider issues and topics of wider public interest and debate. This has been true throughout the history of film as they are all ultimately products of the times in which they are made.

Right and wrong. A major 'public' theme that follows on directly from a 'private' one concerns the discussion of right and wrong. The effectiveness and fairness of the legal system is often called into question here. How far should the hero go? Can he break the law? Can he kill his enemy?

Discrimination. As Superheroes are a very small, admittedly powerful minority, the differing aspects of discrimination and the treatment of minorities are a common theme.

Class. What we refer to as class in the UK is the more simple distinction of rich and poor in the largely American Superhero movie. The heroes themselves come from diverse backgrounds from the super-rich Bruce Wayne through multiple middle-class X-Men to the much poorer Peter Parker.

Science and technology. Our relationship with these two, particularly our suspicion and distrust of them, has been ever present in Superhero movies. In the original 1960s comic books it was the fear of nuclear radiation that spawned many heroes and villains; these days it is the cutting edge science of genetics that is the source for many narratives.

Society. The Superhero movie touches on many other areas of society that are sometimes the subject of our fears and suspicions. Our occasional disquiet at war and the military often leads them to be portrayed as both deliberate and unwitting protagonists. Economics and politics can feature too; Aunt May has her house repossessed in *Spiderman 2*.

The widest kind of public theme is **ideology**. As most of the Superhero movies are American their national ideology is ever present, aspects being:

- American leadership and supremacy.
- The 'pioneer values of the old west' and the 'cult of the individual' – an individual takes it upon themselves to 'make a difference'.
- Freedom – another cherished American value – is used as a justification and talking point in some of these films.
- Terrorism and government attempts to combat it through limiting its citizens' freedoms.

Key terms

Discrimination
Unjustifiable treatment given to different people or groups.

Ideology
A system of values, beliefs or ideas that are common to a specific group of people. All movies will have these, often whether they like it or not.

QUICKFIRE
9

Do Superheroes have to make any choices that are similar to the ones you might be making at this point in your life?

TASK 7

Can you match one or more Superhero movies to each public individual theme?

Daredevil with ninja assassin Elektra in a tangle of both public and private 'issues'

II: Marketing the Superhero

Marketing a blockbuster movie such as a Superhero movie is the job of the distributor. For films of this scale it is as important as the production. In simple terms if no one knows about your movie why would they go and see it? Marketing is the process involved in telling people about movies, and importantly persuading people to go and see them. In order for a film to be successful it is vital that it is sold to us effectively. Movie marketing is the art and science of convincing consumers to buy movie tickets.

There is a strong inter-relationship between production and distribution. Key decisions at the pre-production stages will be made on the basis of what market research tells the producers will be successful. This can be as simple as trying to repeat previous successes but will take in more detailed research such as testing and polling audience responses. The process of finding out what people want, developing a product to meet this desire, and then selling it to them is vital when making and selling films. In terms of the Superhero movie this process includes studio attempts to find the next big multi-million dollar franchise success.

When it comes to selling the movie to the audience a whole range of traditional methods are used. These could be:

- Teaser posters, released very early with a simple intriguing or eye-catching image.
- Posters, whether one sheet or quad the key image used to sell the movie containing all the important information about the film.
- Billboards, large dramatic often inventive images from the film.
- Bus 'T' posters, simple and striking containing release date and review quotes.
- Magazine and newspaper advertisements, based on the poster.
- Teaser trailer, early footage to get the 'buzz' going on the film.
- Trailer, main moving image promotion across multiple media outlets.
- TV spots, shorter versions of the trailer.
- Radio spots, audio only versions of the trailer.
- Cast appearances, TV, radio, Internet interviews.
- Premières, the red carpet, the 'razzmatazz' element to the buzz.
- Merchandise and tie-ins, toys, books, novelties, video games often key to targeting specific markets.

Warner Brothers make a classic tease at ComicCon 2013 with this poster

An inventive approach to billboard advertising

Just a small selection of the
merchandise available for *Iron Man 3*

- Sponsorship and partnership deals, fast food, cars, soft drinks using the marketing of these other companies to promote the film.
- And others!

In the exam you will need to discuss how these are designed to generate interest and persuade people to go and see the film. Indeed each of them may be used to appeal to different sets of people, families, fans, young, old, male, female and so on. These groups are referred to as the different market segments for the film. Blockbusters try to appeal to as many people as possible to get the biggest audience they can. When these are used together, it is referred to as a campaign. The studio hopes this coordinated effort will create the much needed 'buzz' around a movie and highlight that all-important opening weekend, which can be the springboard for box office success (or failure).

Quickfire 10

What are the basic components of a film poster?

Exam tip

Make sure you address the different ways in which producers target specific audience groups.

Keeping the 'buzz' going with an
all-star première gathering

Online marketing

Online marketing has become a vital part in selling a movie, from official websites though social media and viral campaigns. Much of the modern target audience has a significant online presence, particularly on social networks; this means that marketing via the Internet has become more and more important. Much of the early '**buzz**' around Superhero movies begins on the Internet with fans. Speculation and reaction to aspects such as casting and storylines creates a lot of interest. It can become a news story itself when there is a lot of reaction to stories. For example, the casting of Ben Affleck as the next Batman, which generated lots of comment and criticism in the **fan** community.

There are many ways studios attempt to get people interested in their movies, listed below are some of the main ones.

Websites

The 'traditional' way of promoting a movie is the official website. This includes the basic information on the film, often with exclusive or first look content, with links to social networks to increase the exposure of the movie.

The official homepage of the *Kick-Ass 2* website

Social networks

All modern films will have an official studio-created presence on Facebook, Twitter, Youtube and others. This allows the fans and audience to get more involved in talking about and spreading the word on movies. It is the starting point for viral campaigns. Like the official website they often offer exclusive content and interactive ways of increasing the pre-release excitement (or 'buzz'), shown below is the twitter page for the recent *Kick-Ass 2* movie.

Viral marketing

Viral marketing is a more recent form of online marketing. As its name suggests, the aim is to create content that will be spread by the users of the Internet. The viral marketers 'plant the seed' and the curiosity and connections between the fans does the rest. Rather than the studios paying lots of advertising fees seeking out the audience, the content is such that the audience seeks it out themselves. A successful viral that started its impact offline was for the low budget Superhero movie *Chronicle* (2012). The studio hired the viral marketing company Thinkmodo who came up with the idea for a stunt linked to the film, and flew (like the film's teenagers) radio-controlled model people over the skies of New York. It 'went viral' after the footage was posted on the Internet and mainstream news media picked up the story. It was hugely successful as the publicity it generated for the film was far beyond any budget they had for advertising. The full story can be watched in a short video on the site Thinkmodo.com Chronicle (2012) viral:

Launching the 'flying people'

Some of the media outlets that featured the viral

Key terms

Buzz
The amount of collective activity, chatter or 'noise' surrounding the release of a movie.

Fans
The audience that has a greater level of involvement or interest in a film than the average spectator.

Viral marketing
Items that spread like a virus from fan to fan or media outlet to media outlet. They are passed from one to the other motivated by interest and curiosity.

QUICKfire 11

How do you hear about movies – is it mainly online?

Exam tip
Try to think of you own ideas for 'virals'.

12: Exam skills

Question 1

The micro analysis – unlocking meaning on screen

In the exam you will be asked to apply what you have learned about the use of film language to a 3-minute sequence chosen from a Superhero movie. There are some things you should remember to do in approaching this task. Your knowledge of the 'micro' elements of film language is being assessed in this question so be prepared to **identify** them accurately and then explain how they are used.

Specimen micro analysis question

1. (a) Identify **one** special/visual effect used in this extract. (1)

    (b) How is the special/visual effect used in this extract? (2)

    (c) How are **two** of the following used to create excitement in this extract:
    - use of camera
    - sound
    - editing
    - mise-en-scène? (7)

    [10]

Note taking

Before starting to answer the question you will have to view the extract and make notes. You could even set out your notes under headings based on the questions.

Look at Ben's notes, he had 3 minutes to read the questions carefully and then he watched the opening sequence from *Spiderman* (2002) once. He knew from reading the questions carefully that he must concentrate on special/visual effects for 1(a) and 1(b). After the first viewing he decided to focus on camera and sound for 1(c). During and after the second viewing he listed special effects examples to choose from so he could pick the one that best helped him with 1(b) as well. Noting that Q1(c) asked for a discussion of 'excitement' as an audience reaction, Ben listed several exciting aspects of the extract and focused on how camerawork and mise-en-scène helped to create this excitement.

Ben's notes

SFX – Green goblins travelator, SM's web, destruction big buildings, men to skeletons, flying (Spiderman & G.G.)

Camera – long establishing shot – start sequence. Why? Shows cityscape, gg's arrival on travelator, people small, carnival going on.

High angle shot – middle sequence during fight. Mary Jane hanging from ledge, together with close-ups on GG and SM's faces.

M.O.S. – Thanksgiving, Crowds, carnival, balloons, bright clothes, floats, big buildings. Typical celebration to be disrupted by villain.

Costume, weapons, props during fight on ledge.

Part (c) of the question looks at the sequence overall, the most important of the two as it is worth 7 out of the 10 marks. Pay close attention to what you are asked to do. Only discuss two of the four options, there isn't space, time or marks to do more. Pick a feature you consider as exciting and use the correct terminology to help you say why. Try to make sure you choose different (at least two) examples for each, you could also talk about how the two aspects work together to create the nominated meaning. Avoid just describing the sequence.

Question I: Ben's answers

1a. The destruction of the balcony of the big building where Mary Jayne is standing.

1b. The balcony is destroyed bit by bit so the audience sees Mary Jane's growing panic as it begins to crumble and huge parts of it fall into the street below. Visual effects show her clinging to the ledge by her fingertips whilst Spiderman and Green Goblin smash into the glass window behind her.

1c. Camerawork and mise-en-scène work together in this sequence to create excitement. It opens with a typical celebration. It's Thanksgiving and the city streets are filled with happy people dressed in bright clothes, there are balloons, and carnival floats. An atmosphere of general excitement is conveyed through the mise-en-scène. However, the audience experiences a different kind of excitement because they know this is a typical peaceful situation when people's enjoyment is about to be disrupted by the arrival of the villain. An establishing shot follows which shows the New York cityscape. This shot heralds the arrival of Green goblin on

TASK 8

Watch the 3-minute extract from *Spiderman* 2002 used for last year's examination. Compare your answers with Ben's.

Exam tip

Look for the specific meaning you are being asked to analyse. If you are asked to say how excitement is created, this should feature strongly in your answer, not other meanings you may have previously practised.

Exam tip

Remember always keep focus on the meaning you have been asked to discuss. Use the correct terminology when explaining how specific examples help to create this meaning. Show the examiner how you can use what you have learned.

his travelator and raises the level of excitement within the audience. We know a big fight is about to start between protagonist and antagonist — people and buildings are about to be destroyed.

Later in the sequence excitement grows as Mary Jane is trapped on the balcony. High angle shots highlight the distance she has to fall from the ledge, these are intercut with close-ups which show the rising level of panic and fear in MJ's face, and focus on parts of the building as they break off from the balcony.

Examiner comments

Ben answers these questions well. He doesn't waste words when answering the first two parts of the question. He focuses on two or three examples for Question 1(c). He describes how costume, props and setting make meaning in a specific part of the sequence. He considers how atmosphere and audience response are created through mise-en-scène. He accurately identifies three different shots and their uses, again referring directly to the sequence. He consistently comes back to 'excitement' and the ways in which the two elements of film language selected create this response.

Question 2: Identifying, describing and analysing genre codes and conventions

This question is designed to assess your response to genre elements of study. You should demonstrate your understanding of both the 'micro' and 'macro' elements of film language in your answers to the three stepped questions.

Specimen macro question

2. (a) Identify **one** Superhero movie character used in this extract.   (1)

   (b) What makes this character typical?   (3)

   (c) Explain how this character is used in other Superhero
        movies you have studied.   (6)
                                                                          [10]

Like Question 1 you will be asked to discuss one specific point and one of a wider nature. Again try to give a prominent example in part (a) that you can then develop in part (b). In the question above be careful to choose a character whose typicality you can discuss in part (b). What makes them typical is if they are a clear type that can be readily found on the list in the character codes and conventions.

In part (c) you should explore how this character type is used in Superhero movies. You will be expected to discuss examples where they take a similar role to show how they have become a typical character. You should also try to highlight any differences in the part they play, to show how film-makers use aspects of genre to tell their own stories. Most often you may be discussing heroes or villains. Even in the case of these archetypes be aware that they are not all exactly the same. For example, Spiderman and Captain America are both Superheroes, they dress in predominantly red and blue costumes and try to help people and thwart the villain, all typical aspects. However, a major difference that adds some interest is that Spiderman gets his powers through an accident and is not really prepared to take on his role and responsibility. Whereas Captain America has volunteered for his role and is more than ready, indeed his bosses hold him back from the front much to his frustration.

Remember, especially in the longer answers, to try and demonstrate through using examples of your own, that you have thought about how the genre conventions work and have been used in different films.

V pauses to consider the increasing complexity of his symbolism

Questions 3 and 4: Marketing in action

In the exam, Questions 3 and 4 will focus on your knowledge of industry and genre. You will need to apply what you have learned to existing movies and ideas of your own. The first task for this will be Question 3; this assesses aspects of the marketing and promotion of films.

> 3. How are Superhero movies marketed?
>
>   You may refer to the resources material to help you.   [10]

This is quite often the shortest question in the exam that asks the most of you. There are several things to consider when answering this question:

- It is a marketing question so you should discuss how various examples are supposed to work in attracting an audience. Who do they appeal to and how?

- Talk specifically about Superhero movies, use examples from both the resource material and your studies to do this.

- As a blockbuster each example is part of a wider campaign and your answer should reflect this. Discuss the timing of certain types and how they all work together.

- Effectiveness and cost given the size of the budgets involved is also a factor to discuss.

- The need to generate a huge audience to be successful and the smaller market segments that make this up should be considered.

- Above all **avoid two things**: just describing the resource material and giving an answer that could be about any genre of movie.

The second task is Question 4. Not only will this test your industry knowledge but it will look at how you combine it creatively with your genre understanding. In 2013 candidates were asked:

4. You have been asked to create a Superhero for a new movie. Complete the following tasks:

    (a) Choose a name and a special power for your Superhero. (2)

    (b) Explain why you have chosen this special power. (4)

    (c) Design and annotate the homepage for a website featuring your Superhero. Consider:
         - Superhero movie conventions.
         - The layout and design of your website homepage. (8)

    (d) Explain how your website will help to sell your movie. (6)

    [20]

There are three key things to remember when approaching a Question 4:

- Industry and audience knowledge and understanding.
- Genre knowledge and understanding.
- Creativity and imagination.

The examiner will want to test your understanding of how the film industry works and uses genre and conventions but as important at this stage is to try and be creative. You can use ideas you have had before, come up with them in the exam but whatever you do, try and make your answer at least a little different from existing Superhero properties. Never be afraid of being different especially as you will have chance to explain your ideas to earn the higher level marks.

For example in (a) and (b) try to come up with a unique selling point (USP) for your hero. When you explain in (b) remember that a power is more than just a narrative device, it can say something about the character, have a visual impact on screen and in marketing and be an important part of the wider franchise.

Part (c) is usually the design element of the question and the two bullet points are there to remind you what the examiner will principally be looking for. Although it is not a test of your artistic skills, some attempt to visually illustrate your ideas, even using typical colours, will improve your chances of covering both bullet points. You should also remember that annotation is not just labelling but a chance to explain how your design will work as a tool to sell your film, try not to miss this opportunity. Part (d) most times follows on from this. You should try to take at least three key features and explain how they will target a specific audience, spread the word or persuade people to go and see your movie.

Overall the most important thing to remember when dealing with marketing is how it builds on and uses the features of the genre to increase the tickets sales for these expensive productions that need the largest of audiences to make them financially worthwhile.

Quickfire answers:

1. Since the dawn of the blockbuster movie with *Jaws* (1975) and *Star Wars* (1977) they have been the dominant model of film making for the big studios. It has become a proven way that the studios can earn very high levels of revenue based on high levels of investment. The earnings from these franchises are what support the production of many smaller projects. This is why they are sometimes referred to as 'tent poles' as they hold up the rest of the studio's activities.

2. It is important for many reasons. It provides a rich source of material for their screenplays in terms of both character and plot. It is the pre-sold element that both fans and the general public already know and recognise. Less positively, it can represent a balancing act as the fans can be very protective of their favourite character's history and too radical a change to it in its journey to the screen can mean negative buzz around the movie.

3. Other popular genres could be comedy, sci-fi or horror. These remain popular as they are clearly defined genres with many years of established codes and conventions. Film-makers know what to do, audiences know what to expect and perhaps most importantly distributors know how to sell them.

4. There are not many. Often where New York isn't mentioned then it is a place that looks a lot like it. Even DC's Metropolis is a fictional version of New York. It is filmed on the fringes of the main Superhero universes that tend to be set elsewhere. Sometimes it's for budgetary reasons and often it's to differentiate their movies from the 'Big 2'. *V for Vendetta* is one example; *Chronicle* is set in Seattle and *Hancock* in Los Angeles.

5. The answer here lies in the differing qualities and demands of the two media. Comic books traditionally use colours to maximum impact in order to stand out from the competition on the newsstands. Even the designs of the costumes sacrifice practicality and realism to the need to look striking and cool. The visual demands on film are different. If audiences are to accept the story and 'suspend their disbelief' then a degree of realism or believability needs to be present. The bright primary colours and minimal coverage of the drawn characters don't physically work, or look too 'cartoony'. So inevitably many costumes translate only the essence of the comic book look. Although as the genre becomes a more accepted and longstanding part of the cinema world, costumes have moved closer to their comic book originals. And as audiences become more familiar with Superheroes they become willing to accept more of the less realistic elements.

6. Interestingly neither. The comic book series began first as Mark Millar collaborated with John Romita Jnr. Jane Goldman and Matthew Vaughn started the screen play after the comics but completed it before the comic book series was finished, so both forms contributed to the original Kick-Ass story.

7. There is no definitive answer here but, like some of the longer questions in the exam, the mark you get depends on the quality of your argument in applying the codes and conventions. Another key factor will be what you consider to be a hero, do you prefer a darker or a more archetypical approach. My answer here would be Spiderman. He has an iconic costume, cool powers, started as a teenager, which I originally connected with; he is powerful but not so distantly powerful as the alien Superman or the super-rich Batman two other contenders for this title.

8. There are not many as, like most genre-based movies, the studios like to keep it simple and linear so as not to alienate the mainstream audience. There are some examples that are at least partly cyclical, *Daredevil* (2003) starts partway through the story with the injured hero crashing to the floor of the church, *Kick-Ass* (2010) starts with a voice-over that looks back to how it all began and at one point references other films where the narrator is already dead such as *Sunset Boulevard*. Interestingly, if you watch the deleted scenes on the *Avengers Assemble* (2012) extras, the unused opening scene is of Agent Maria Hill looking back on the events of the film and giving her opinion on the events, if this had been used it would have made the narrative much more cyclical.

9. This links to the Superheroes that are teenagers like Spiderman and the mutants in the X-Men films. They have many of the problems associated with this age group to contend with: growing up, life choices, physical changes, self-image and how they will fare in the adult world; very similar but magnified with the extra dimension of superpowers.

10. Title, tagline, star(s), director, strong main image, billing block, release date, positive critic quotes.

11. It depends... a good way to start any longer explanation question. Younger or more fan-based audiences will tend to actively seek out things they are interested in online. This does not rule out having your 'eye caught' by more traditional posters, billboards, bus T, TV and magazine-type advertising.

Section 4: Paper 2 – Exploring Film Outside Hollywood

I: Introduction

Paper 2 is an examined unit of GCSE Film Studies. This unit involves the close study of one film produced outside Hollywood, chosen from the list below:

Amelie, Bend It Like Beckham, The Devil's Backbone, The Wave, The Boy In The Striped Pyjamas, Persepolis, Yasmin, Rabbit-Proof Fence, Ratcatcher, Tsotsi.

In this section you will explore the important key areas you will need to study in terms of your focus film. Examination questions are based on **four** main areas of study:

- The characters, narratives, themes and issues in your chosen film.
- The issues raised by the chosen film.
- The representation of people, places, events and issues.
- How film language contributes to those representations.

A creative question will allow you to talk about:

- Your response to the film.
- How other audiences have responded to the film.
- How it uses film language.
- What it says about other people, places, events.
- Who made the film and why.

A number of films will be considered in order to allow you to focus on specific areas in your film. Each case study contains advice on the ways in which you should analyse and express your understanding of how meaning and response are created by the micro and macro elements of film language.

Exam tip

Make sure you know something about the making of your film, e.g. director, writer, actors. Talk about their previous work or why they wanted to make your film. Be prepared to make comparisons with other films. Think about the differences and similarities between your focus film and films made in Hollywood.

Hollywood

Hollywood is a district in Los Angeles, California, famous for its commercial area and entertainment industry. It is also the name used to represent the motion picture industry of the United States. Films made in Hollywood usually have:

- Enormous budgets
- World famous stars
- Marketing 'muscle'.

They dominate the world market and make it very difficult for the film industries in smaller countries to compete. Because Hollywood is so sophisticated, rich and powerful the films made there attract huge audiences across the rest of the world. They take a huge slice of film box office profits. So it can often seem that the local, cultural voices of lower budget films made elsewhere in the world are overwhelmed by the might of the 'Hollywood machine'. For example, here in Great Britain our local multiplex cinemas typically serve up one 'blockbuster' after another. Many are based on well-known literature, ensuring that they sell well across the world. Your study of the Superhero genre will have made you aware of the huge popularity of such films. These films contain all the pulling power that Hollywood can muster: big stars, big budgets and mind-blowing special effects, their stories are based on comics and graphic novels that already carry a significant, 'ready-made' fan base.

The list of focus films includes films that were made in: Australia, South Africa, Mexico, France, Germany, Iran and Great Britain. When we talk about films made outside Hollywood we perhaps assume that films made in these countries are quite different to Hollywood cinema. This isn't necessarily true; the style, setting or actors may be quite different but there may well be striking similarities. So, for example, *Tsotsi* may have been a low-budget film featuring several 'non-actors' but it was based upon a novel and it does contain many of the conventions of a Hollywood gangster film. It is really important therefore to make sure you know some key facts about the production of your focus film and have compared it with a Hollywood production. What similarities are there? What differences are evident? What does the film tell us about the place, time and culture in which it was set?

The following sections all focus on different films from the set list. Each case study is divided into five areas:

Introduction – the film's social and historical context, and background information about its production, exhibition and distribution.

Places – the representation of settings and their relationships to key themes and issues.

Events – the representation of events. Narrative structure, time and space, viewpoint.

People – the representation of characters and their relationships to key themes and issues.

Creative response – expressing your understanding of the film.

An exemplar Paper 2 with guidance on answering Questions 1 and 2 is at the end of this section.

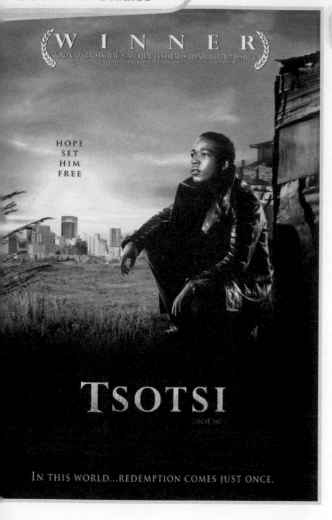

2: Studying *Tsotsi*

Introduction

Tsotsi was made in South Africa and released in 2005. The story is set in the township of Alexandra situated just outside Johannesburg. It was awarded an Oscar for the best foreign film in 2006. This was seen to mark an important turning point for the South African film industry which had previously received its financing from other countries (predominantly America) in order to produce films in English featuring Hollywood stars.

South Africa is a land of great contrasts. It is stunningly beautiful and contains great natural wealth in the form of diamond mines. It is also a land affected by terrible poverty, disease (HIV AIDS), poor housing and high crime rates. It has had a turbulent history. Apartheid, a racist system of segregating the black indigenous population from the white ruling classes, was introduced in the late 1940s. It was not abolished until the 1990s. Athol Fugard, a prominent South African playwright, wrote *Tsotsi* in the early 1960s. His short novel was set in Apartheid South Africa. Gavin Hood, the film's young South African director, also wrote the screenplay. He decided to set the story in the 21st century because sadly, the problems of racism, poverty, poor housing and disease have not gone away.

3: Places – setting, themes and issues

This section will explore how settings in *Tsotsi* contribute to our understanding of the themes and issues in the film. Setting is an important signifier of the film's themes and issues. You will know, for example, that poverty is an issue in this film, but need to ask yourself how Hood conveys this. There are stark differences in settings in the film.

Consider the shack where Tsotsi lives and compare this to the baby's home. How does Gavin Hood show these differences? Think carefully about how the mise-en-scène helps make meaning.

Task 1

Look at the screen stills and annotate aspects of the mise-en-scène which highlight the differences between Tsotsi's bedroom and the baby's.

Tsotsi changes the baby's nappy with newspaper!

The baby's bedroom

Don't ignore what the director shows you. Everything in the frame means something and will have been carefully considered – nothing is coincidental. For example, look at the prevalence of the AIDS sign that seems to frame the crane shot of the railway station below. This is Hood's way of explaining to the audience what kind of society Tsotsi lives in – one that is rife with disease.

The bustling city station

There are a number of significant locations within the film, each of these locations relate closely to narrative themes. They are:

- Alexandra township
- Tsotsi's shack
- Soekie's Bar
- Miriam's home
- Pumla's house
- The pipes
- Johannesburg.

Quickfire

1

What issue is presented by Hood in the image of the pipes?

Exam tip

Good answers will analyse the ways in which this scene connects with other moments in the film to create a coherent view of a particular issue.

The little children sleeping in the pipes at night

79

Make a chart like the one below to help you make links between the settings in your chosen film and how they convey certain themes or issues.

> **TASK 2**

Setting	Themes and issues	Evidence?	Light and colour
Tsotsi's shack	Poverty Crime	Lacks basic comforts Cramped – one room Contains stolen goods	Dark Low key lighting Shadows Monotone – browns
Miriam's home	Family Hope	Clean, neat, tidy Homely Nicely decorated Care	Bright Natural light from windows Fresh blue walls Colourful mobiles reflecting light
Pumla and John's house	Wealth Disparity	Electric gates Modern conveniences Spacious	Electric light High key lighting Fresh Sophisticated decor

The locations help us understand the characters and themes and issues.

Now look at the three stills that follow. Think carefully about what Gavin Hood wanted to show in each of these settings. The shanty town where Tsotsi lives is important. It is big and heavily populated – this is shown in a crane shot as we see the town sprawling for miles into the distance. A haze envelopes the township, suggesting a polluted environment. The buildings are ramshackle and mostly made from scrap materials. Some of them appear to be on the point of collapse. Tsotsi's shack is constructed from corrugated metal and is dark, dimly lit, and full of shadows; it seems to symbolise his state of mind. It is important to make links between location and themes and issues. The poverty so clearly shown in the environment clearly contrasts with the wealth and security of John and Pumla's home.

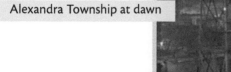

Alexandra Township at dawn

Tsotsi's home: dirty, dark and ill equipped to look after the baby

Miriam's home – clean, comfortable and bright in contrast

QUICKfire
2

Look carefully at the stills of Miriam's and Tsotsi's homes. How do these setting relate to the themes or issues of your chosen film?

Tsotsi deals with many issues:

- Poverty
- Crime connected to poverty
- The disparities in wealth across Johannesburg
- The threat of HIV/AIDS to the country
- The power of redemption.

For each of these find one screen sequence that illustrates the issue well and explain how the director highlights this issue.

Are any of these issues highlighted more clearly because the story is set in South Africa?

TASK 3

Micro and macro elements

You need to constantly be able to refer to both the **macro** and **micro elements** of film when analysing the relationship between locations and themes/issues. For example, in *Tsotsi*, a 'macro' issue is poverty, but what sequences in the narrative help convey this issue? Think about the 'micro' details that Hood uses – the queue for the water standpipe, the makeshift homes, the children living in the pipes, the sprawling,

Key terms

Macro elements
The overview, the big picture, the themes and issues.

Micro elements
The zoomed in, little details that help convey the macro. These include the elements that make up the mise-en-scène.

81

densely populated township all help the audience understand that Tsotsi lives in a poor area of Johannesburg. The start of the film shows that the gang live in a poor area, have few opportunities and turn to crime in order to survive. The sequence at the railway station shows how far they will go in order to get money. It helps to illustrate the way themes and issues are linked – the gang turn to crime because they live in poverty.

Miriam helps an elderly neighbour at the water standpipe

4: Events – narrative, themes and issues

This section will help you to identify and explore how key events in *Tsotsi* help to drive the narrative. It also considers the importance of narrative construction and the ways in which it can contribute to our understanding of the themes and issues in the film.

TASK 4

Create a timeline of events in the film (using post-it notes) so you have a visual overview of the narrative. You could use different colours to highlight areas of tension or development. This will help you spot narrative devices such as Tsotsi's flashback to his childhood and help you consider why the director has chosen to use these conventions. For example, consider Hood's use of the flashback device to 'fill in' Tsotsi's back story. This helps you to understand Tsotsi's behaviour and attitude. Did you have more sympathy for him once you knew his mum had died from AIDS and his father broke his beloved dog's back?

Narrative is the film's story and the way in which it is told. Narrative structure is the way in which the narrative is ordered and organised within a film.

- Linear narrative – one that runs in a straight line from beginning to end.

- Cyclical narrative – one that ends where it began – it moves in a cycle.

- Episodic narrative – one that has separate stories that are linked together.

TASK 5

Consider Tsotsi's narrative construction – look at the shape of the text from your timeline. Is it linear? Cyclical? Episodic?

Let's explore the importance of the pipe scene once again; this time in terms of narrative structure.

Young Tsotsi (David) seeks refuge from his abusive father in the pipes

This scene comes nearly half-way into the film, but shows where Tsotsi has come from. Although mostly linear in structure, Hood also uses a flashback device to take us back to Tsotsi's childhood so we have a more comprehensive understanding of his character. The effect of using this narrative technique is to help show that Tsotsi was not born a hard-hearted thug, but sadly, he is a victim of terrible circumstances. He deserves our sympathy and quickly earns it when we witness his mother dying of AIDS. Tsotsi's previous conversation with Morris, *'What kind of man would kick a dog?'*, makes sense now as we watch, alongside the young David, his dog being kicked to death by his alcoholic and abusive father. Everything seems to be against David as he runs away in the pouring rain and has to seek shelter in a sewage pipe with other homeless people. So here we can see how Hood uses a certain technique to link the narrative with the themes and issues in the film – those of family, disease and poverty.

It's no coincidence that near the beginning of the film the camera tracks Tsotsi walking along the track from the train station. Think of the film's narrative like a journey – Tsotsi's personal journey from callous crime to redemption.

Tsotsi leaving the city station after his confrontation with Morris

Exam tip

Think about **key sequences**. In the exam, you might be asked to refer to key sequences in your chosen film, so have some ready to draw upon.

83

In terms of revision it is important for you to be able to identify key moments in the development of the narrative of the film and think about what moves it forward; an incident? A character's behaviour? The decisions of a group?

Task 6

Prepare a PowerPoint for your class selecting key sequences or at least stills from them. Be prepared to justify why these sequences are important and how they help convey the key themes and issues within the narrative. For example, key issues in *Tsotsi* are poverty and redemption, but what sequences in the narrative help show this?

Task 7

Find micro examples of these macro issues:

- Crime.
- Wealth.
- Disease.

When analysing this sequence it is useful to pause at key moments and think about the way film language is giving us important narrative clues about characters or themes. For example, look carefully at the still below. This close-up tells us a lot about Tsotsi, the dead man's face is right at the front of the frame and Tsotsi's appears almost pushed up against it. This tight framing excludes any possibility of Tsotsi escaping the full horror of what has just occurred. The lighting accentuates the horror and fear in his eyes, his mouth is open as the shock at what Butcher has just done sinks in. This is the first time his expression has shown any kind of emotion, we see that whilst he may be a thug, he is not a 'Butcher' and the possibility of redemption is signalled.

Tsotsi realises the enormity of Butcher's attack

Exam tip

Choosing an appropriate key scene is very important. When you are asked to do this in the exam make sure you spend time thinking about your choice and do not talk about the whole film in your answer.

Narrative and character development

The representation of key events, character development and the narrative structure combine to explore or express important themes and issues within the film. The narrative structure allows us to discover more and more about Tsotsi as his story unfolds.

We are constantly challenged in our assumptions about the central character. By analysing events such as the murder in the opening sequence we are given clues that our initial impression of Tsotsi as a thug may change. The use of flashback within the narrative structure allows us to understand why he behaves in the way he does.

Tsotsi thanks Miriam for her kindness

Key events gradually allow us to learn more about him and how social issues such as poverty can affect behaviour. They also provide important 'turning points' within narrative. For example, when Tsotsi sits at Miriam's table and says 'Thank you' (see still above). Two simple words of gratitude combine with the other micro elements of film language to highlight a profound change in the central character, and to signal the final stages of his journey towards redemption. It is at this point in the film where Tsotsi realises what it is to love and care for someone else and perhaps here he begins to understand the meaning of decency.

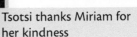

- Look at Tsotsi at the beginning of the film. How is framed? How is he lit? What is his body language/facial expression like? How does he behave? How does he interact with others?

- Consider him again near the end of the film. How has he changed? Is he framed differently? Has the lighting altered? Is his body language/facial expression different? How about his behaviour and interaction with others?

- Try to pin down what events in the narrative have brought about these changes.

5: People – character, themes and issues

This section will explore how characters are represented in *Tsotsi* and the ways in which they interact with key themes and issues. Gavin Hood, the film's director, used a mixture of actors and non-actors in his cast. Presley Chweneyagne (Tsotsi) and Terry Pheto (Miriam) had both lived in poor townships just outside Johannesburg so they had experienced, in real life, some of the hardships that faced the characters in the film. Hood's aim was to create characters that were as realistic as possible and to try and avoid the overuse of simplistic stereotypes so often employed within Hollywood films.

Stereotypes are often used as a shortcut in film (as time is restricted so characters can't be 'fleshed out' as in a novel or TV series) so an audience can quickly identify their 'type' and make certain assumptions about them.

Exam tip

You are studying Film, not Literature. Yes, knowledge about characters and plot construction is important, but we want you to consider the visual/aural language used, not the written word. So, always ask yourself HOW a character or place is represented in terms of mise-en-scène which includes:
- Props, costume
- Lighting
- Body language
- Framing.

Tsotsi gestures to Fela who ridicules him for not having a car

Props

Props are often important signifiers of a character's personality or motivations. In the examination you may be asked to 'identify an important prop used by a character in your chosen film'. It can be useful to pause your DVD at a moment where you think particular props help to define a character or characters. For example, the still below of Boston.

Boston getting drunk in Soekie's Bar

Boston is a failed teacher and subsequent alcoholic. To make this very clear to the audience, Hood has him clutching a beer bottle in most of the early scenes so the audience can quickly identify what kind of character he is. His small, steel-rimmed glasses are also important. He is the only character that wears glasses. He is a reader, he can add up, he has had an education. They perhaps signify that he is the only one in the gang who can see clearly. He has morals and can see right from wrong. Perhaps the bottle helps to numb his conscience. When his glasses are destroyed in the fight with Tsotsi he becomes a broken man. He has lost his vision actually and metaphorically. Similarly, Butcher carries with him a menacingly sharp bike spoke so we identify him as violent and dangerous. He is seldom seen without a weapon and his refusal to listen to Tsotsi and the end of the film may signify he is beyond redemption.

Costume

Costume can be an important signifier of character. When considering its use you should describe the costume and make an attempt at explaining how the costume contributes to our understanding of the character. A good answer will go further, though, both in detailed description and in analysing how this links to a wider understanding of the issues raised in the film.

Fela telling Butcher to work with him, not Tsotsi

Lighting

Lighting is important in terms of how a character is represented. For example, Tsotsi is often framed by shadows. At the beginning of the film, he is rarely in high key lighting, tending to lurk in half-lit areas of the set. Notice how the top lighting of the frame below accentuates his hooded eyes making him appear sinister.

Tsotsi staring at Boston just before he attacks him

Think about how lighting helps convey character. Miriam, for instance, is always lit with natural and high key lights because she is a 'light' character – she has nothing to hide and lives a good life. Remember, it is not enough to **describe** the lighting: the question asks you to **explain**, and the best answers will **analyse** – by making connections between this element and themes and issues in the film.

Quickfire 3

Look at the still on the left and use it to answer this question:

Explain the use of costume worn by a character in your chosen film.

Exam tip

Describe the use of costume and then **explain** how this contributes to the characterisation. Good answers will **analyse** the way in which this contributes to an audience's understanding of themes and issues in the film.

Framing

In the opening sequence we immediately understand Tsotsi is the central character of the film because the camera always focuses on him. Hood uses lots of close-ups of Tsotsi's expressionless face to help us understand his complex character.

The extreme close-up (below) makes the audience feel close to Tsotsi but also uncomfortable because we are so near to him and he seems dangerous and someone to beware of. His dead eyes give us no clue to his thoughts and make us position against him. Later on, Hood pulls out from these kinds of shot to much wider, more balanced frames as Tsotsi begins to embrace the world around him and our initial feelings are changed as we come to feel sympathy for him.

Are stereotypes used in *Tsotsi*? If so, how are they identified? What makes them adhere to the stereotype? What props, costumes, lighting, etc., are used to represent them? Look at this typical 'thug'. Consider his pose, expression, costume and the lighting.

Tsotsi spots his victim

For revision purposes, you might like to create a grid like the one below to have an overview of characters and their representations.

Character	Costume	Representation
Tsotsi	Black leather jacket Hoody Red converse	Thug Gangster Yob 'Hoody'
Aap	(Stolen?) Prison overalls – property of…	Criminal Suspicious Henchman
Miriam	Gold-coloured cardigan Traditional African dress Headdress	Respectable Motherly Clean, neat, tidy
Fela	Sharp 'zoot' suit Open neck purple shirt Gold chains	A 'player' Gang boss Businessman

The best Film Studies answers are specific, practical and give a sense of the visual. Below is a checklist containing some of the visual elements of film language which are used in the representation of Tsotsi at the beginning of the film:

- He is the leader of the gang. This is immediately established in the opening sequence when we get a close-up of his face and the camera tracks him, not the others.

- He is centrally framed with members of his gang following on each side of him.

- He is an angry young man. This is shown by his very **serious facial expression** and his swagger. He is not afraid to give Fela (a much more powerful gangster) a rude gesture. His coldness is conveyed through frequent **close-ups** of his emotionless eyes.

- He is a criminal. His black hoody is an important piece of costume because it helps create a 'shortcut' to his character. Because of popular media representations, we associate young people wearing hoodies with crime and anti-social behaviour.

Tabloid newspapers often refer to young people as 'hoodies' and use it as a catch-all term for disaffected youth. So, having Tsotsi wear a black leather jacket and hood helps us identify him as someone to mistrust.

Exam tip

Almost everybody watches films. What you've got to do in this exam is separate yourself from the ordinary consumer of film and define yourself as a film expert. So, you need to load your answers with film terminology and enjoy showing off all you've learnt about film craft.

Tsotsi returning the baby to his rightful home

But Tsotsi is a changed person at the end of the film. His costume helps to accentuate that change: He has been 'redeemed'. When he takes the baby back he wears a smart, clean, white shirt. It symbolises his redemption; he has come good and has learnt the value of love. The white signifies a sense of hope as Tsotsi has literally 'come clean' and is ready to face the consequences of his actions.

When you consider how important **mise-en-scène** is to our understanding of this character in a key sequence of your chosen film, you should look carefully at:

- Setting
- Costume
- Lighting and colour
- Body language.

Key term

Mise-en-scène
Literally what is 'put in the frame'.

Think about the meaning behind Hood's direction – Tsotsi's body language is hunched; he's looking down at the tracks and looks troubled. He is heading back to the township following the tracks as if he can't deviate from the life he has been given.

Tsotsi heading back home after the confrontation with Morris

Tsotsi's black leather jacket and hoody help him to fit into this dark environment, almost as if he is connected to the dark side of the city and the crime and violence there.

The setting, the lighting and Tsotsi's costume are all dark, which helps set the serious tone. Consider the effect if this scene had been shot in bright daylight.

Lighting is low key. The scene is set at night so shadows are prominent and there is a feeling of foreboding.

Character development

Throughout the film our attitude to Tsotsi changes, we see his character developing and learn more about him. You may be asked in your exam to explain the ways in which this development is shown, e.g. 'How and why does the central character in *Tsotsi* change?'

This is a longer question, requiring you to show a wider knowledge of the film and to **describe** key moments, **explaining** their significance, and then **analyse** the meaning that they make when seen as part of the whole. Many students will answer 'how' well, but only the best answers will show an appreciation of 'why'. The best answers will show awareness that Tsotsi changes not just because of the narrative forces in the plot, but because the director wants us to see hope amid the bleakness of the townships.

Think about what Tsotsi learns. How does his learning help you in your understanding of the film's message? Interestingly, Hood also directed the Superhero film, *X-Men Origins: Wolverine* in 2009. Hood said about *Wolverine*:

'Any movie that is simply about good versus evil...is in my view putting out into the world and certainly into a mass audience and young audience's mind a rather dangerous philosophy, which is that there is good and evil in the simplistic and easily defined way....' (Wikipedia)

Below is an example of Tsotsi from the beginning of the film. He is represented as a dark character, he is top lit and looks menacing. His facial expression is serious and he looks tense and ready for a fight. The dialogue (subtitles) even spells out what kind of person he is initially.

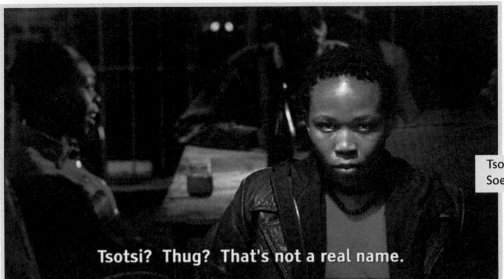

Tsotsi? Thug? That's not a real name.

Tsotsi stealing for a fight in Soekie's Bar

This is the starting point for Tsotsi's journey, although we later come to realise that the starting point came much earlier in his life due to a lack of love and exposure to cruelty as a child. Does Hood need to add this detail of Tsotsi's life? You could discuss whether it helps the audience start to feel pity for Tsotsi, when we have been given little else to like until that point.

Later in the film, Tsotsi's hard exterior begins to soften. In the frame below, he is lit by much softer, natural light, is surrounded by cosy, colourful home comforts and his facial expression conveys more emotion – this half smile is the first time we see him derive pleasure from anything.

This hard 'thug' develops into someone who cares for a baby, helps his friend and is able to thank people for their decency. Tsotsi's experiences have changed him. He has matured in a very short space of time by learning to think about others before himself. At the end of the film he is ready and able to face the consequences of his actions and we, the audience, feel that for Tsotsi his future will now be a positive one.

Tsotsi relaxes in Miriam's home as David is fed

Tsotsi hands over the baby and surrenders to the Police

Revising *Tsotsi*: creating a mind map

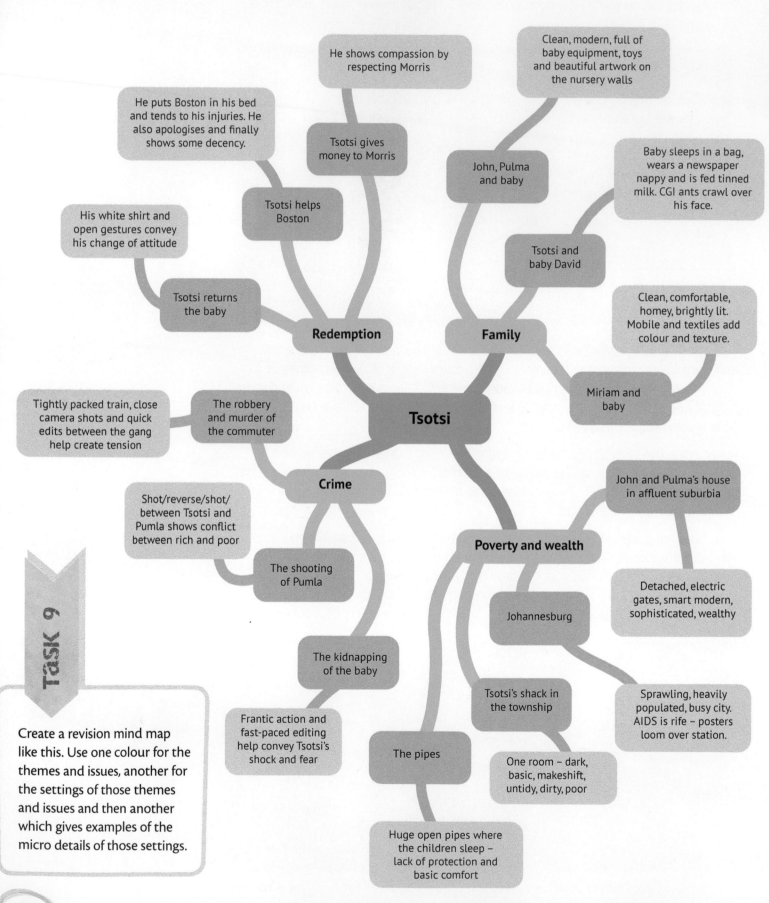

He shows compassion by respecting Morris

Clean, modern, full of baby equipment, toys and beautiful artwork on the nursery walls

He puts Boston in his bed and tends to his injuries. He also apologises and finally shows some decency.

Tsotsi gives money to Morris

Baby sleeps in a bag, wears a newspaper nappy and is fed tinned milk. CGI ants crawl over his face.

John, Pulma and baby

Tsotsi helps Boston

His white shirt and open gestures convey his change of attitude

Tsotsi and baby David

Tsotsi returns the baby

Clean, comfortable, homey, brightly lit. Mobile and textiles add colour and texture.

Redemption

Family

Miriam and baby

Tightly packed train, close camera shots and quick edits between the gang help create tension

The robbery and murder of the commuter

Tsotsi

Crime

John and Pulma's house in affluent suburbia

Shot/reverse/shot/ between Tsotsi and Pumla shows conflict between rich and poor

The shooting of Pumla

Poverty and wealth

Detached, electric gates, smart modern, sophisticated, wealthy

Johannesburg

The kidnapping of the baby

Tsotsi's shack in the township

Sprawling, heavily populated, busy city. AIDS is rife – posters loom over station.

Frantic action and fast-paced editing help convey Tsotsi's shock and fear

The pipes

One room – dark, basic, makeshift, untidy, dirty, poor

Huge open pipes where the children sleep – lack of protection and basic comfort

TASK 9

Create a revision mind map like this. Use one colour for the themes and issues, another for the settings of those themes and issues and then another which gives examples of the micro details of those settings.

6: Exam practice – creative response

Question 3 – Exploring, responding, evaluating

This question may ask you to write a review, blog, respond to a message board, etc. Have prepared what you want to say about the film – this is your chance to air your own opinions and show off your knowledge and understanding of the film. Prepare for this by reading lots of film reviews so you understand the style, tone, content, etc. *Empire* magazine/empireonline, *Total Film*, *The Guardian*, www.bbc.co.uk/blogs/markkermode are all excellent resources to use.

Below is a review of *Tsotsi* found on *www.empireonline.co.uk*

Exam tip

For your personal response to Question 3, try to refrain from just describing your chosen film as 'good' – it becomes meaningless if overused. Try to have a bank of adjectives you might use to describe the text: effective, thought-provoking, moving, exhilarating, enigmatic, depressing!

Director's name

Very brief summary

Genre

Actor's name

Opinions re: narrative

Summative opinion

Comparisons with other films

Personal response and audience reaction

Aspects of film language

Performance

Gavin Hood's third feature has inspired comparisons with City Of God, yet his harrowing look at six days in the life of a Soweto thug who accidentally kidnaps and grows attached to a tiny baby shares the weary compassion of last year's Crash as much as the brutal desperation of Fernando Mereilles' acclaimed hit. Hood cleverly interweaves elements of psychological thriller with a complex, layered character study, as Tsotsi (first-time actor Presley Chweneyagae) struggles to cope with his new companion, and the police close in on his trail. At times it's a difficult watch; the lead character is borderline psychotic in his inability to empathise with those around him, but it's testament to Chweneyagae's outstanding performance that such a frightening individual is understood and embraced by the audience, even as his actions repel. Shot largely in desaturated, sepia tones in Soweto's claustrophobic shanty towns, the raw energy of Tsotsi's existence is in neat contrast to the wealthy couple whose baby he has stolen. While some scenes (flashbacks to Tsotsi's AIDS-blighted childhood) are rushed and a little clumsy, Hood handles his material so deftly that a conclusion which could have been mawkish and sentimental is instead bittersweet, both painful and quietly affirming.

Verdict: With lively pacing, superb performances and a candid yet forgiving heart, Hood has created an inverse fairy tale that is never less than absorbing.

Reviewed by Liz Beardsworth

Exam tip

Don't re-tell the story – it wastes time and only shows you've watched the film. Favourite parts – have them ready and explain why. How does this film compare to others? Is it better or worse?

TASK 10

Although the questions change every year, you know you are going to be asked your opinion of your chosen film. Practise writing a review for yourself and then someone who hasn't seen the film; for your friends and then your teacher. Experiment with different modes of address.

Improving exam responses

Look at this student's answer and the examiner's advice on how they could stand out more as a film expert.

This is a decent start – the candidate offers their personal and honest response to the film. They could show off a little though and specify who made *Tsotsi*, when and what kind of budget it had compared to Hollywood films they had seen.

> Tsotsi is a great film and I haven't seen anything like it before. At first, I was worried I wouldn't like it because it was South African and had subtitles and I am used to only watching Hollywood films but I was really surprised by how much I enjoyed this film.

Here the candidate shows understanding of the film's themes and issues but is rather general in their approach. They could expand on **how** the film deals with issues of poverty and crime by giving specific examples. There is a great opportunity here to use film language knowledge. They could write about how Hood establishes the issue of poverty with his wide crane shots of the makeshift township. They could quickly explain how they knew that the area where the baby lived was middle class and wealthy because of the smart electronic gates and security system, for example.

> This film deals really well with a range of issues like poverty and crime and helped me understand that some young people are forced to turn to crime (like Tsotsi) because they are so poor. I also learned that Johannesburg is a city which is both poor and wealthy. I was surprised to see that just over the hill from Tsotsi's township was a very middle-class and wealthy area where the baby lived.

Look at all the missed opportunities to explain **how** Tsotsi is represented as a thug – they could focus on his costume, body language, facial expression and give short examples from sequences in the film.

> At the beginning I hated Tsotsi because he was a real thug and never seemed sorry for what he had done. I thought he was really cruel to Morris and couldn't believe it when he shot Pumla. I was really scared he was going to kill the baby.

Again, there's a chance here to explain **how** and **why** Tsotsi's performance was realistic and **how** he changed (through costume, body language, facial expression). This could also be improved by perhaps explaining that Presley Chweneyagae (who played Tsotsi) and Terry Pheto (Miriam) were both non-professional actors who had lived in similar townships to the one depicted in the film.

> I think the actor playing Tsotsi was really good as he played a very realistic thug at the start but then changed for the better. I thought his performance was excellent. I also thought the actress who played Miriam was really pretty and suited playing the role of a kind mum.

A really important point is made here but only briefly – this needs exemplifying with some specific examples of **how** and **where** colour is used and what effect it has. It's also not enough to just say the lighting is brighter – an explanation of **how** is necessary.

> Film language is used in the film to highlight themes such as redemption. For example, the film gets more colourful when Tsotsi meets Miriam and the lighting is brighter near the end to show that Tsotsi has changed for the better.

Exam tip

Show off! You've studied this film for a long time – let us know what you've learnt. What knowledge have you gleaned from independent research like reading reviews or watching the DVD extras? How do you personally feel about this film? Hopefully, your study of this film will have been a positive experience – tell us about it!

7: Studying *The Devil's Backbone*

Introduction

The Director of *The Devil's Backbone*, Guillermo Del Toro, was brought up in Mexico. He made films from being a child though he started his career in the film industry working on special effects and make-up. He even had his own company in this area for 15 years. He produces, writes novels and screenplays and is also a talented artist.

Though he has specialised in horror films; *The Devil's Backbone* and his more recent film, *Pan's Labyrinth*, explore the fantasy world of children alongside brutal acts of the Spanish Civil War.

Mexico is one of the most violent countries in the world today. It is a place where there are many social problems. Though his films may not be about Mexico or these social issues, it is evident that Del Toro's cultural background affects his work and that the issues that he deals with in this film are universal. *The Devil's Backbone* is a supernatural thriller set in an orphanage haunted by the ghost of a young boy. It follows in the tradition of important films which have explored the legacy of the Spanish Civil War from a child's point of view.

8: Places – setting, themes and issues

This section will explore how settings in *The Devil's Backbone* contribute to our understanding of the themes and issues in the film. Setting is an important signifier of the film's themes and issues. You will know, for example, that isolation and entrapment are key themes, but you need to be able to analyse how Guillermo Del Toro uses film language to convey these themes. There are at least three significant locations within the film. Each of these locations relates closely to narrative themes. They are:

- The Spanish Plain – isolation, entrapment, abandonment.
- The orphanage including: courtyard – abandonment, spirit world, waiting, conflict. Classroom – group unity, solidarity. Dormitory – spirit world, group conflict, isolation. Carmen's bedroom – desire, power. Casares' bedroom – unrequited love, **impotence**.
- The cellar or **cistern** underneath the orphanage – revenge, the spirit world, entrapment.

Key terms

Impotence
The inability to act according to your desires (could be physical, emotional or sexual).

Cistern
An underground reservoir for rainwater.

Pick one key sequence for each significant setting. Make notes on how the 'micro' elements of film language convey important themes or issues in each sequence. See below for some ideas on the importance of the Spanish Plain.

TASK 11

Opening sequence of *The Devil's Backbone*: Carlos is driven across the Spanish Plain towards the orphanage

The film opens as Carlos is being driven across the vast Spanish Plain towards the orphanage. It is so hot the abandoned wrecks of old vehicles appear to move like dying animals in extreme heat. The black car looks tiny surrounded by this huge open space. The amber colour palette emphasises the burnt nature of the countryside. There are no signs of life, the sun beats down relentlessly on the dry, dusty land. We learn later that the nearest village to the orphanage is at least a day's walk away. Mise-en-scène suggests that this is an 'unforgiving', hostile environment. Ideas about entrapment and isolation are clearly signalled.

TASK 12

Make a chart like the one below to help you make links between the settings in your chosen film and how they convey certain themes or issues.

Setting	Themes and issues	Evidence?	Mise-en-scène
The Spanish Plain	Entrapment, isolation, hostility	Opening sequence. Hot, dry, dusty. Huge space with no buildings, animals or birds. Surrounds the orphanage so there is no escape.	Amber colour palette emphasising the heat. Long shot which makes car look almost 'ant-like'. Shimmering heat makes abandoned bits of metal appear to move like dying animals. High key lighting emphasising the brightness and intensity of the sun.
The classroom	Group solidarity Abandonment	Carmen's lesson on mammoths. Children all focused on lesson in which Carmen teaches the benefits of strength in numbers/working together.	Old-fashioned classroom, desks in rows. Picture pinned to a board. Carmen with stick points to pictures of woolly mammoths. Long shot from back of the class showing the backs of the children's heads. All looking towards Carmen at back centre frame. Above her head is the dusty outline of where a crucifix once hung, perhaps suggesting God can't help them so they must help themselves.
The cistern			
The dormitory and other bedrooms			
The courtyard			
The village			

The Devil's Backbone: Carmen teaches the boys a lesson on group solidarity

The orphanage

This is the most important location in the film, all the characters are 'enclosed' in this environment – it is where the major part of the narrative action takes place. Each of its rooms highlights narrative themes. The building serves a whole host of different purposes:

- It's an orphanage and a school. The children of republicans killed during the ongoing Spanish Civil War have been sent there to be cared for and educated.
- It's a place of safety hidden away from the violence and bloodshed.
- It's a 'prison'. The nearest village is a day's walk away so the children are trapped, there is nowhere for them to escape to.
- It's a place which holds secrets, spirits and ghosts.

In terms of representation we don't see much of the outside of the orphanage. Most of the action goes on in the courtyard or the rooms inside. All of these spaces hold secrets. In the bedroom Carlos is given Santi's bed and locker. How he died is shrouded in secrecy.

Santi reveals himself to Carlos in the basement but holds on to his secret until almost the end of the film. Even the cupboards keep secrets, providing a hiding place for Carlos after he first sees Santi and for all the boys leading up to the final confrontation with Jacinto. As the narrative unfolds the secrets of these locations are revealed one-by-one.

What secrets are hidden in the kitchen and the courtyard?
Which secret is kept from the boys at the end of the film?

The cistern a room full of spirits, secrets and shadows

Genre

Your work on the Superhero will have already revealed the strong relationship between genre and narrative. There are typical narratives and settings that we have come to expect once we identify a particular genre. The representation of the orphanage suggests the Gothic horror genre. Typically Gothic horror films feature a dark castle set in the middle of nowhere. This building has dark, winding corridors, hidden recesses, gloomy basements – secret places inhabited by all kinds of 'unearthly beings' such as vampires, ghosts and spirits. Typically, during the day the building appears relatively normal, although there are clues that all is not as it should be. However, at night the corridors and recesses become dark, forbidding spaces full of shadows, sighs and shocks.

TASK 13

Re-watch the short sequence which shows Santi's first night visit to Carlos in the dormitory (0.16.24 – 0.18.52). Make notes on the ways in which the 'micro' elements of film language help to create a forbidding place 'full of shadows, sighs, shocks'.

The kitchen contains the secret hiding place for Republican gold. Jacinto's actions are largely driven by his desire to find the gold and escape the orphanage. The courtyard encloses the huge rusting bomb. We are told at the beginning of the film that it has been defused but it still ticks, it seems know the secret of Santi's death and in one scene its flag appears to point the way to the basement so that Carlos may also discover the secret.

The ghost of Casares follows the boys to the orphanage gates at the close of the film. His existence is revealed to the audience but the boys are not aware of his presence as they begin their long journey towards the challenge of living in a fascist-controlled Spain.

9: Events – narrative, themes and issues

This section will help you to identify and explore how key events in *The Devil's Backbone* help to drive the narrative. It also considers the importance of narrative construction and the ways in which it can contribute to our understanding of the themes and issues in the film. *The Devil's Backbone* is a social and political commentary as the story takes place at the end of the Spanish Civil War. It is a tale of revenge, greed, and the thin line between the world of the living and the world of the dead. The recurring images and symbols throughout the film reinforce these themes.

Narrative structure

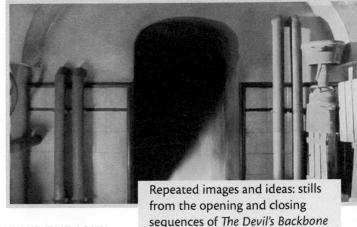

Repeated images and ideas: stills from the opening and closing sequences of *The Devil's Backbone*

WHAT IS A GHOST?   *A TRAGEDY CONDEMNED TO REPEAT ITSELF TIME AND TIME AGAIN*

In an interview just after the release of the film Del Toro said that his film was '*about a big war but contained within a small war*'. He felt that the best way to convey this **duality** was to have an opening and an ending that were 'similar but different'. He wanted to repeat ideas and images but each time adding something to them. This technique gives the audience a different perspective on people, places and events within the narrative.

The film begins with an opening and closing **montage**.

> Re-watch the opening and closing montage sequences.

Task 14

Below is a table charting the images that make up each of the montage sequences:

Opening sequence	Closing sequence
Image of a doorway	Image of a doorway
Falling bomb	Santi hovering over the pool of water
Injured boy	Wreckage of orphanage *dissolve to*
Boy drowning in pool	Jacinto drowning in pool *dissolve to*
Jaime, covered in blood at pool side	Bomb in courtyard *dissolve to*
	Boys leaving the orphanage *dissolve to*

The final shot is of the ghost of Casares as he watches the boys on their final journey towards 'civilisation' and whatever Franco's new Fascist regime holds for them.

Each montage sequence is accompanied by a voice-over. It is Casares' voice and he repeats the same questions but in the final sequence two extra sentences are added, 'A ghost. That is what I am.'

Below is a checklist which lists some of the narrative purposes of the images used in the opening montage. You may want to add your own ideas about each image in terms of meaning and response:

Key terms

Duality
Denoting two persons or things.

Montage
A series of images that are somehow connected.

QUICKFIRE 6

Why are the two extra sentences added?

99

- Image of the doorway – the way into the story? Voice-over introducing issues of repeated tragedies and the nature of ghosts.

- Falling bomb – links idea of repeated tragedies, war and death.

- Injured boy lying by poolside – creates an **enigma**, a puzzle to keep audience interest, who is the boy, who has injured him?

- Figure drowning in pool of murky amber water – enigma continues, is it the same boy? It's hard to see. If it is, then a murder has been signalled. Water seen as a tomb (an enclosure to receive dead bodies).

- A boy covered in blood, head in hands squatting by the pool – theme of secrets introduced. Because the audience constantly seeks to make sense of images and to link them together into a story, we assume this boy has a guilty secret.

Key terms

Enigma
A puzzle.

Motif
A repeated symbol.

Benign
Kindly, friendly.

QUICKFIRE 7

What meanings are communicated by the liquid in Carlos' laboratory jars?

So stylistically, this montage creates a powerful mysterious way of introducing ideas about the ways that tragedies are repeated, of war, of ghosts, of secrets and murder.

Motifs recur throughout the film in a variety of situations:

- The image of the bomb is returned to repeatedly.

- The pool that will eventually hold two dead bodies.

- Casares, laboratory jars containing deformed foetuses.

These motifs also perform an important role in the narrative. The bomb is a constant reminder of the Civil War that was just entering its final few months. It had been disarmed, like so many of the republicans, but its heart continued to beat. Jaime says, '*You'll hear it ticking. That's its heart. It is still alive and it knows we are here*'. Certainly, it does seem to have life of its own, its presence seems **benign**; it appears to signal the way for Carlos to find Santi.

It's worth re-watching the sequence where we finally find out what happened to Santi (1.14.11 – 1.20.00) as a part of your revision process. If you analyse how the narrative organises key events within the film and notice the ways in which repeated images (motifs) are used you will clearly see how they underline important issues. The sequence begins as Jaime begins to tell his story to Carlos. They are both sitting on mattresses in the dormitory. The story starts with a typical storytelling/flashback device, as he says 'I saw everything' his image dissolves and the conversation also 'dissolves' to become a narrative voice-over.

Jaime begins his story

The cross-dissolve takes us from one place to another and hands over the storytelling role for the first time to Jaime. We already know that the cistern is a key location; it is where Santi reveals himself to Carlos. The opening montage shows the pool, recurring motifs feature or suggest its murky amber water. As Jaime dissolves, the image of the water resolves, suspending him in pool for a split second. It is an important element of both the tale he is about to tell, and the film's continuing story.

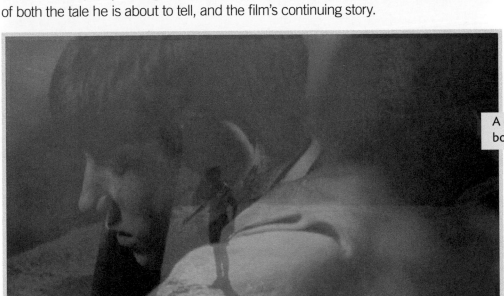

Quickfire 8

What is the pool's significance in the film's continuing story?

A cross-dissolve: Jaime touches the bomb and finishes his story

Quickfire 9

Del Toro uses a series of cross-dissolves to show Jaime walking towards the bomb at the end of this sequence. What effect do these have? Why do you think his final dissolve shows Jaime touching the bomb and then returning to his story in the dormitory?

Task 15

Below is a list of three key narrative events. Analyse one of these events in terms of narrative structure and importance.

- The bomb dropping.
- Carlos' arrival at the orphanage.
- Carmen's lesson on how mammoths were hunted.

10: People – character, themes and issues

This section will explore how characters are represented in *The Devil's Backbone* and the ways in which they interact with key themes and issues. It is useful to note how Del Toro stretches the conventional uses of editing techniques throughout the film with the frequent use of dissolves. These typically encourage the audience to make connections between the dissolving and resolving images, but Del Toro also uses them to expand time and create ghostly presences for some of the characters. Posing the question, are all the characters ghosts 'suspended in time like a blurred photograph'? Del Toro also uses sound not just to create atmosphere but to highlight the visual and physical representation of his characters.

Exam tip

Typically representation is analysed by looking closely at mise-en-scène. Make sure you also consider editing and sound when exploring how Del Toro presents his characters.

Carmen watches Jacinto and Conchita embracing: she becomes another ghostly presence in the dormitory

Quickfire 10

Describe Carlos' body language and costume in the opening sequence. Explain how this contributes to your first impression of this character.

The narrative begins with the arrival of Carlos at the orphanage. He is the main protagonist. Some of the narrative unfolds through his eyes but not all. Casares' voice-over at the beginning and end of the film suggests he has an important role in telling the story and Jaime's flashback allows him to recount the story of Santi's death. The opening sequence gives us a lot of information about Carlos:

● He wears a blazer and is carrying books. The other boys wear open-necked, soiled shirts. They are clearing rubble from the courtyard or chasing chickens.

● He has an inquisitive nature. He is constantly looking around, taking in all he sees. He immediately goes to check out the bomb.

● He does not know that he is about to be left at the orphanage.

An inquiring mind: Carlos knocks on the outer casing of the bomb

The still above highlights an important element of Carlos' personality. He is not frightened of the unknown. He immediately makes physical contact with the bomb. Throughout the narrative Carlos connects with the spiritual world; ghosts and even objects (the bomb) help him. At the beginning of the film Carlos is frightened and lonely. He is bullied by the other boys, especially Jamie, but his courage and persistence not only means he makes friends but that he also faces up to Santi and helps to save a lot of the boys.

For revision purposes, you might like to create a grid like the one below to have an overview of characters and their representations:

Character	Representation	Themes/issues
Carlos	Inquisitive, brave, persistent, 'in tune' with spirit world, helps others to change.	Spirit world, isolation, courage, revenge, abandonment.
Santi	A ghost, a murder victim, seeks revenge, can see into the future.	Entrapment, revenge, waiting, spirit world, abandonment.
Jaime	Eldest boy, initially a bully, a coward who changes to become more sensitive. Finally leads the other boys, avenges Santi's death.	Conflict, revenge, group solidarity, courage, abandonment.
Jacinto	An orphan with dreams of becoming rich and powerful. The villain who tries to steal the Republican gold.	Power, greed, abandonment, conflict, entrapment.
Dr Casares	The school's Science teacher and doctor. Kind, bonds with Carlos. Loves Carmen, talks of revolution but is impotent – unable to act on his desires.	Impotence, waiting, science vs spirit world, war, self-sacrifice.
Carmen	The school principal – a fighter, protecting orphans and the gold. Maternal – teacher and mother. In constant pain – strong sexual needs.	War, courage, isolation, conflict, self-sacrifice.
Conchita	Beautiful, innocent. Loves Jacinto but is also afraid of him. Shows selflessness and courage at the end. Gives her life to protect the orphans.	Love, courage, isolation, self-sacrifice.

> **TASK 16**
>
> Choose three of these characters. Select a short key sequence for each and analyse how the 'micro' elements of film language contribute to their representation.

Though the narrative has the Spanish Civil War as the backdrop to the film, the isolated nature of the orphanage means that much of the typical imagery and action associated with war is largely absent. Instead, different characters and events represent elements of the war; and the story of the ghost symbolises aspects of Spanish society. The orphanage is run by Republican sympathisers, it is the hiding place for Republican gold and the children of Republican fighters. The audience are placed in a sympathetic position to their cause. Jacinto seems to represent the fascists, as he bullies the children, kills Santi and uses his position to try and steal the gold Carmen is hiding.

QUICKFIRE 11

How does mise-en-scène in this still tell us important things about Jacinto?

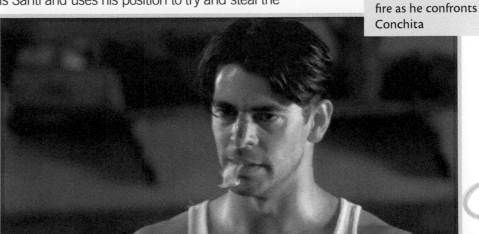

Jacinto breathing fire as he confronts Conchita

Representing a ghost

The relationships between characters within the film are important. Carlos is clearly the main protagonist but it is Santi who is at the centre of the intricate web of relationships represented:

The changing nature of Santi's ghost: beginning

- He guides Carlos (and the audience) to the truth about his death.

- He discovers Jacinto when he tries to steal the gold for the first time.

- He warns Carlos that 'many will die'.

- He helps the children to prevent Jacinto from escaping with the gold he has been planning to steal for quite some time.

- He enables Jaime finally to take his revenge on Jacinto for both his and Conchita's death.

When creating Santi, Del Toro works within the traditional conventions of the ghost story. In an old building there lives a ghostly figure that haunts the current inhabitants of that place. This ghost will not rest until the circumstances of his death are uncovered or avenged. Below is a checklist containing several of the key ways in which he uses film language to heighten Santi's effect on the audience:

The changing nature of Santi's ghost: ending

- The haunting sensations are heightened through the isolated setting and by enhancing the otherworldliness of the ghostly apparition with low key lighting and a deep blue/grey colour palette.

- Ghostly sounds signal Santi's presence even when he cannot be seen. His sighs also alert the audience and the other characters that he is somewhere near, hiding in the shadows. When he speaks, his voice is child-like but it echoes faintly; the sound of water dripping is also layered onto his voice.

- An unsettling sensation of being observed is established as the spectre is always seen looking at Carlos from dark thresholds, keyholes and basements.

- Santi leaves frightening signs, such as footsteps on wet floors and a terrifying trail of blood in the air.

- The camerawork also creates a sense of gliding through time and space.

- Tracking/dolly shots are used to create a smooth seamless feeling. Cross-dissolves also create fading, ghost-like figures.

Initially Santi is only seen for brief moments but as the story and plot unfold he becomes more recognisable as another orphan reveals himself to Carlos for longer periods.

QUICKFIRE 12

Why has the sound of water dripping been layered into Santi's voice?

11: Exam practice – creative response

Question 3
Talking about your film

Question 3 is your chance to demonstrate just how much you know about your focus film and to consider the effect it has had on you. It allows you to focus on a number of different areas so you can clearly evidence the knowledge and understanding gained through the close study of your film:

● How particular themes or issues affected you.

● What you learnt about other people and other places by studying the film.

● How it compares with other films of the same genre, or with similar themes.

● What you know about the production, distribution or exhibition of the film.

● How film language is used in the film.

You should come to this question with a ready-made 'fact file' in your head. This fact file should contain information that you have found interesting/informative – information that may have affected your response to the film. Below is an example of a 'fact file' for *The Devil's Backbone*:

Exam tip

If you are asked to explore film language you need to consider 'micro' or 'macro' elements NOT dialogue!

Country of origin	Mexico 2001
Setting /social historical context	Orphanage in the middle of a Spanish Plain. Spain, 1930s during Spanish Civil War between Republicans (Carlos, Carmen, Casares) and Nationalists (Jacinto).
Director and/or screenwriter	Guillermo Del Toro – Mexican director, screenwriter and producer of *Devil's Backbone*. Is also an artist and novelist. Has alternated between Spanish-language dark fantasy pieces, such as *The Devil's Backbone* (2001) and *Pan's Labyrinth* (2006), and more mainstream American action movies, such as *Blade II* (2002), *Hellboy* (2004), and *Pacific Rim* (2013).
Key characters	Young – Carlos, Jaime, Santi, other orphans. Older – Carmen, Casares, Jacinto and Conchita.
Actors	Marisa Paredes (Carmen) and Frederico Luppi Casares – two of Spain's most famous actors. Luppi has also worked on several of Del Toro's other films – similar role in *'Chronos'*.
Genre	Gothic horror set during Spanish Civil War but contains universal message about 'lost generations' of young people throughout history.
Style	Editing – use of dissolves, Flashback to Jaime's story. Cinematography – Santi appears at night, low key lighting, shadows, sighs (sound), and blue, black, grey colour palette. Daytime amber colour palette, heat, dust, ideas of entrapment. Dolly shots which create a gliding ghostly feeling. Representation of Santi.
Film language	Go back to your analysis of a key sequence. Pick out effective 'micro' or 'macro' comments.

TASK 17

Create your own 'fact file' for revision purposes.

Let's look at excerpts from a good student response to Question 3.

This is a terrific opening paragraph. The student considers director, his influences, and his body of work and compares *The Devil's Backbone* with Del Toro's most critically acclaimed film. She doesn't simply name the film but demonstrates an understanding of themes and issues in both drawing parallels and pointing out differences in both narratives. Words have not been wasted re-telling the story, she goes straight into a consideration of the bullet-pointed areas.

Del Toro's 'Devil's Backbone' is a personal piece accompanied by another one of his movies, 'Pan's Labyrinth'. Both films deal with the Spanish Civil War and the effect that war has particularly on children. However, 'The Devil's Backbone' is more cynical than 'Pan's Labyrinth' as the children lose their innocence through war and Ophelia, the main character in 'Pan's Labyrinth' does not to the same extent.

Later she goes on to consider narrative, themes and issues. Again she is succinct, words are not wasted, every point she makes gains her marks. Her ideas are beautifully expressed and convey a sense of constantly searching for meaning.

'The Devil's Backbone' leaves everything unresolved: the boys are still on their own and the ghosts are still trapped at the orphanage. This is deliberate though as Del Toro feels that the Spanish Civil War is still unresolved for many. The movie addresses the theme of war. In the town scene prisoners are led out into the courtyard, blindfolded and shot, showing that like animals being led to the slaughter the human race will go blindly down the path of war again and again.

The student concludes her response with her personal response. Again this response is justified/evidenced by close reference to the film's language.

It's nice to see a film which has themes about war without war being in your face, so to speak. Del Toro is subtle and it pays! It's also refreshing to see a ghost that is not a threat and children that are portrayed as complex characters. Hollywood seems to be missing that these days.

TaSK 18

Practise writing an opening paragraph that deals with at least two of the bullet pointed areas of focus; a central paragraph that considers one or two different areas; a concluding paragraph which involves personal response to the themes, characters or style.

12: Studying *The Wave*

Introduction

The Wave is a German film made in 2008. It is based upon a real-life experiment carried out by a young teacher called Ron Jones in 1967. Jones was working at a High School in Northern California. When working on the political and social background of Germany during the Second World War, he began to question how it was possible for German citizens to claim, after the war, to have known nothing about the Holocaust. His attempt to answer this question as a new teacher in 1960s California led to a risky experiment into fascism that has intrigued successive generations ever since. Ron Jones went on to write a short story about his experiences. The screenplay for *The Wave* is based upon his storybook. However, *The Wave* (*Die Welle*), is not set in California but in modern-day Germany. It is a cautionary tale about the roots of fascism. It highlights the importance of education but also underlines concerns about the roles and responsibilities of a teacher. The director, Dennis Gansel, stated that he was anxious to explore what makes a perfect teacher, and to examine what effect they could have on students. *The Wave* won a German film Award for Outstanding Feature Film and Best Supporting Actor (Frederick Lau) in 2008.

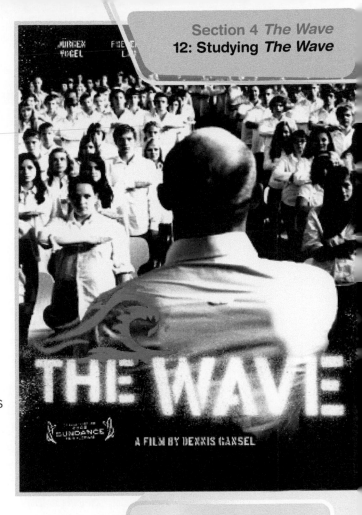

13: Places: setting, themes and issues

This section will explore how settings in *The Wave* contribute to our understanding of the themes and issues in the film. Setting is an important signifier of the film's themes and issues. You will know, for example, that power and education are key themes, but you need to be able to analyse how Dennis Gansel uses film language to convey these themes. There are several significant locations within the film, each of these locations relate closely to narrative themes. They are:

- The school and the classroom – education, power, peer pressure, group vs individual rights, autocracy, **conformity** and **non-conformity**.
- The assembly hall – **autocracy**, **dissidence**, peer pressure, power.
- The swimming pool – dissidence, peer-pressure, group vs individual rights
- Rainer Wenger's houseboat – conformity and non-conformity.

Key terms

Conformity
An action or behaviour that fits in with the established way of doing things.

Non-conformity
Actions or behaviours which go against the 'normal' or established way of doing things.

Autocracy
Dictatorship or absolute rule by one person.

Dissidence
Disagreement with the established government.

> Pick one key sequence for each significant setting. Make notes on how the 'micro' elements of film language convey important themes or issues in each sequence.

TASK 19

The classroom is clearly an important setting. Rainer Wenger begins his classes on autocracy there on Day 1 of project week. As he walks in it is clear from the body language of the students that they are not particularly interested in the subject. Most

Mr Wenger teaching about absolute rule by one person

of them seem to have taken this option because they like Wenger's teaching style. Key themes are quickly established by the film's language and in his opening discussions with the students. If you look at the still above you will see Wenger is placed firmly centre frame. His arms are outstretched so he almost fills the whole of the frame. The blackboard at the back of him is also in sharp focus and we can clearly read the word 'Autokratie' (autocracy), in fact it almost seems to be coming out of his head like a speech bubble. He is represented as an important, powerful character.

Wenger's students are cynical about the importance of studying autocracy (as was Wenger when given this subject to teach). The discussion reveals elements of racism and ironically, the belief that history cannot repeat itself and that Germany would never be open to the kind of fascism that led to the Second World War.

Rainer Wenger's character allows the audience to look critically at how education can so easily be used to communicate and enforce particular ways of thinking (ideologies). The classroom provides him with a stage on which to use his charisma in order to get his students onside. As the project week progresses he insists on rules and uniformity amongst his students. By doing this, Wenger attempts to show them how the ideas that have propped up particular regimes in the past (Nazi Germany), and the present (North Korea), can easily be communicated within the education system. The fact that he loses control of his experiment underlines how careful teachers should be.

Quickfire 13

How does the mise-en-scène in these two classroom scenes communicate important narrative and thematic changes?

Before: unruly, scruffy, uninterested students (and teacher?)

After: disciplined, uniformed interested students (and teacher)

Make a chart like the one below to help you make links between the settings and key themes and issues in your focus film.

TASK 20

Setting	Themes and issues	Evidence?	Mise-en-scène
School/ classroom	Education, power, conformity, non-conformity, fascism/autocracy	The argument between Wenger and Herr Weiland	Students change into uniform. Karo is isolated for not conforming. Discipline, logos, salutes. Wenger as controlling leader.
Assembly hall	Power, fascism, dissidence, conformity, non-conformity, conflict, group identity	Wenger's final assembly, when doors are locked, students whipped up into a frenzy Violent climax	Stage for Wenger to address his followers. Positions him above them. Depth of focus: students are blurred, standing to attention. Wenger's back in sharp focus almost filling front of frame.
Swimming pool	Conflict, group identity, dissidence	Team initially losing matches because they can't work together. Later aggression directed towards the other team, group works together, becomes increasingly violent	Final water polo match. Pool packed with supporters. Match becomes like a gladiatorial contest with the crowd worked into a frenzy. Underwater sequences, which use slow motion to accentuate the increasing violence.

Wenger addresses his 'followers'

QUICKfire
14

Analyse the ways in which mise-en-scène underlines Wenger's powerful position at this point in the narrative.

The assembly hall

On the final day of the project Wenger, fearing he has lost control of the project, assembles all the students in the main hall. The setting is important; it allows Wenger to 'take centre stage' above the students, enhancing the power he holds over them. The curtains at the back of the stage offer a space for 'off stage activity' between other key characters.

In this sequence, the viewer is placed alongside the students. We may know more than they do but we are not sure what Wenger will do.

14: Events – narrative, themes and issues

This section will help you to identify and explore how key events in *The Wave* help to drive the narrative. It also considers the importance of narrative construction and the ways in which it can contribute to our understanding of themes and issues in the film.

Below is a checklist of the key areas you should note in terms of narrative structure:

- It has a linear narrative.

- The action takes place over the course of a school week.

- Each 'sphere of action' begins with a caption telling us which day it is. This action runs from morning through to late evening. This serves to emphasise just how quickly Rainer Wenger's project takes hold of the students.

The narrative structure is linear – the story begins at the start of the week and finishes at the end. There is a repetition of imagery – Wenger begins his journey to school in his car and ends his journey being driven away in a police car.

Rock 'n' Roll Rainer on his way to school

BASIEREND AUF DER KURZGESCHICHTE
UND ORIGINALPROTOKOLLEN VON
WILLIAM RON JONES

UND DEM DREHBUCH THE WAVE VON
JOHNNY DAWKINS + RON BIRNBACH

With great power comes great responsibility – Wenger leaves school for the last time

The film ends as it began, with Wenger in a car looking out of a window, but it is here that all similarities end. Wenger is no longer in the front seat driving (literally and metaphorically). He is handcuffed and sitting in the middle of the back seat of a police car. As he is driven off, the frames slow as he looks about at the victims. The final shot shows Wenger staring into the distance, his expression suggests that he sees something ahead of him that frightens him, but this something is not revealed to the audience.

Ron Jones, the teacher who carried out the real life experiment in America, has his own theory about the meaning of the final shot. He says that the expression on the face of the teacher at the end of the German film is designed to make the audience, everyone, consider their own capacity for evil. '*It puts it into a universal context. We're all capable of this nightmare.*'

Task 21

Watch the final sequence (01.29.00 – 01.37.16). This sequence carries on from the last (above).

Discuss the following questions:

● How is film language used to show Rainer's downfall?

● Does the ultimate responsibility for what happens in *The Wave* lie with the teacher, or are other factors responsible?

● Compare the opening sequence with the closing sequence. Which differences and which similarities are evidenced?

15: People – character, themes and issues

This section will explore how characters are represented in *The Wave* and the ways in which they interact with key themes and issues.

Representation: the opening sequence

Sound

Sound quickly helps to establish character in the opening sequence. Rainer Wenger (Jürgen Vogel) is driving to his job while passionately singing along to a cover of Rock 'n' Roll High School. The music and lyrics are obviously important in terms of establishing themes. Rainer has his car window open and the stereo speakers are turned up to full volume. When the line 'I don't care about history' is played, a close-up shows his work files being scattered across the car seat. The diegetic music changes to non-diegetic as Wenger arrives at school and crosses the playground into the staff room, again 'I don't care about history' is foregrounded in terms of sound levels. This is a clear indication that attitudes towards school and what is taught there are going to be important in the film.

Costume

The role of history and what it may or may not tell us about the present is a key theme in the film. Wenger is also established as something of a 'maverick'; he is unshaven and wears a Ramones T shirt. Even his first lines of dialogue are aimed to mock the double standards of his fellow teachers who stand by the window smoking: 'Make sure the kids don't smoke in the yard huh?' Critically, the opening scenes of *The Wave* show Reiner Wenger as an anarchist by nature. When he finds he has not been given this project to teach during the school's project week he asks the Head if he can swap with Herr Wieland, another more 'conservative' teacher, who has been given the task. Wenger argues that his background at Berlin University, and his experiences as a squatter and demonstrator, mean he knows more about the subject of anarchy than Weiland. But in a telling interchange between the two teachers Weiland (obviously an establishment figure, denoted by his costume and speech) argues that he is far more able to teach 'the virtues of democracy, not how to make a Molotov cocktail'.

How do costume and body language help to establish character in the two stills below?

Wenger goes to ask for anarchy rather than autocracy

Weiland shows his disdain for Wenger and his teaching methods

For revision purposes you could create a grid like the one below in order to have an overview of characters and their representations.

Character	Representation	Themes and issues
Rainer Wenger	Charismatic teacher, non-conformist, arrogant, powerful, popular.	Non-conformity, fascism/ autocracy, education, power, history.
Tim Stoltefuss	Initially represented as an outsider, an insecure student who has problems at school. Becomes an unquestioning disciple of The Wave. Vulnerable, the 'flaws' in his personality mean that he is easily led. Desperate to 'fit in'. Sense of community and purpose created by The Wave defines his character from day one of the class. His obsession with the movement increasingly envelops him.	Conformity, peer pressure, unquestioning loyalty, group identity, fascism.
Karo	Bright, strong minded, attractive, asks questions rather than obeys orders. Karo and Mona are the only students to recognise the dangers of the project. Tries to effect change from within, becomes increasingly isolated and her relationship with Marco disintegrates.	Education and the ability to question, dissidence, peer pressure, group identity, fascism.
Marco	Good looking, popular, bright, likes to fit in with the crowd but still has a questioning mind. At first doesn't see any connection with their activity and fascism, but in final scene is the only student to question Wenger's actions.	Education and the ability to question, dissidence, peer pressure, group identity, fascism.
Herr Weiland	Old-fashioned, establishment figure, unpopular.	Education, conformity.

Group identity

Rainer's week-long experiment quickly expands outside the classroom. Look carefully at the still below. Both groups of young people are wearing 'uniform' of sorts. The uniform is important because it creates/reflects a sense of group identity.

How does the mise-en-scène in this still suggest conflict between the groups? What are the dangers and advantages of creating a group identity by dressing in a similar way? Why do you think Wenger asked his students all to wear white shirts?

16: Exam practice – creative response

Talking about your film – Exploring, responding, evaluating

Question 3 is your chance to demonstrate just how much you know about your focus film and to consider the effect it has had on you. It allows you to focus on a number of different areas so you can clearly evidence the knowledge and understanding gained through the close study of your film:

- How particular themes or issues affected you.
- What you learnt about other people and other places by studying the film.
- How it compares with other films of the same genre, or with similar themes.
- What you know about the production, distribution or exhibition of the film.
- How film language is used in the film.

You should come to this question with a ready-made 'fact file' in your head. This fact file should contain information that you have found interesting/informative, information that may have affected your response to the film. Below is an example of a 'fact file' for *The Wave*:

Country of origin	Germany 2008
Setting/social historical context	Present day, Germany, large high school. Experiment which looks at the ways in which a powerful, fascist leader can gain power and control a nation. Obvious parallels between the growth of fascism in Germany during the 1930s and Hitler's rise to power.
Director/ screenwriter	Dennis Gansel wrote and directed. German Award for best screenplay.
Key characters	Rainer Wenger, Tim, Karo, Marco.
Actors	Jurgen Vogel (Rainer Wenger) – well-known German actor, singer and screenwriter. Frederick Lau (Tim) – awarded German film prize for his portrayal of Tim. Max Riemelt (Marco), Jennifer Ulrich (Karo).
Style	Pounding score of rock songs and music by Heiko Maile combines with the cinematography of Torsten Breuer to capture the action, especially powerful during the aggressive water polo matches, which incorporate a combination of outstanding hand-held and slow-motion camera work.
Genre	Youth film.
Film language	Fast editing and fluid camera work harmonise with the score to engage a young audience. Classroom scenes strengthened by effective use of fast pans from one student to another, so that we can gauge their reaction to what is being taught. Over-the-shoulder shots allow Wenger's influential presence to loom large at the front of the frame. There can be no escape from his influence.

Now, let's look at some short excerpts from one student's response to a past Question 3.

Hi James, I've just finished studying a German film called *Die Welle*, or *The Wave* if your German's not too hot! It's based on a true story about a guy called Ron Jones who thought he would try an experiment on his students in California. Anyway the experiment went wrong; he lost his job and then wrote a story about it. Denis Gansel, the film director got hold of the story and decided to write a screenplay from it, only he set it in Germany. I guess that's because the experiment was all about the ways in which a really powerful charismatic leader can make people do what he wants them to do.

The opening paragraph adopts a relaxed style but manages to convey quite a lot of information. The source of the original story, country of origin, director's name, the fact he adapted an original story into a screenplay. He also pinpoints a major theme.

I think this film really appeals to an audience our age. It has a great opening, when the teacher, Rainer Wenger (Jurgen Vogel) is driving to school The Ramones' song 'Rock 'n' Roll High School' is blasting in his car and he's singing along – obviously not a typical teacher, especially as he's wearing a Ramones T-shirt, baseball cap and jeans!

A central paragraph deals with target audience, and representation.

I really enjoyed studying this film. It has superb screenplay, direction and great acting from its mainly young cast. I felt myself being drawn into the film in the same way as Mr Wenger's students were being drawn into his 'experiment'. The drama unfolds relatively slowly at first, but with gathering momentum and consequences. There is also a very moving portrayal of some of the tensions produced within some of the romantic pairings as well as the extreme anguish caused in one student by his heightened susceptibility. I think the depth to which personal relationships and social groupings are explored make this into much more of a fascinating drama than an exercise in the condemning of fascism. Please don't be put off by the subtitles. I can't recommend this film too highly.

The final paragraph deals with personal response and HOW this personal response has been shaped by performance, narrative and themes.

This is a good creative response demonstrating a wide knowledge and understanding of a number of suggested areas. It is well expressed with a clear sense of personal engagement.

TASK 22

Watch the alternative ending on the extras. Write a short blog which discusses both endings. You should describe the differences between each ending, say which ending you preferred and why, and consider the reasons for the Director's final choice.

17: Exam skills

Paper 2 – Exemplar examination paper

This section includes some sample questions from the 2010 Paper 2 examination. The paper has been annotated in order to help you achieve the marks available.

Exam tip

Time management can be a problem especially when you have lots to say.
Be very strict with yourself: 10–15 minutes max on Question 1, then 15–20 minutes max on Questions 2 and 3. This should then leave 5 minutes to check through your answers and make a few additions/corrections if necessary.

1. (a) Identify **one** theme or issue from your close study film. (1)

Make sure you accurately identify a theme or issue.

EARLY WARNING ALERT!

Before you choose which theme/issue. Read through parts (b) and (c) to make sure you can both describe, and analyse how they are communicated in a key sequence.

This answer does not require a description. 1 theme/issue = 1 mark

(b) Briefly describe what the film suggests about the theme or issue. (3)

Key word is 'briefly' – 3 marks available – usually 3 brief sentences will do.

EARLY WARNING ALERT!

Don't analyse/consider key sequence here – save it for part (c) below.

You can consider the whole film here. Could there be different 'readings' of themes or issues? What messages and values are conveyed?

(c) How is this theme or issue explored in a key sequence from your close study film? (6)

This question involves looking closely at the ways in which the 'micro' and 'macro' elements of film language help to communicate the key theme identified in 1 (a).

EARLY WARNING ALERT!
DO NOT STRAY FROM YOUR KEY SEQUENCE.

This question is designed to test your ability to closely analyse a particular sequence, to consider how it creates meaning and response and to use appropriate terminology.

Make sure you identify your key sequence and can name people and places accurately.

Total = 10 marks

2. (a) Identify an important setting from your close study film. (1)

EARLY WARNING ALERT!
Read through parts (b), (c) and (d). Make sure you have picked a setting that you can write about in detail.

A 1-mark question – just name the setting.

(b) Briefly describe this setting. (3)

Where is it? What does it look like? Make three clear points. Don't stray on to the next question.

(c) What does this setting suggest to audiences? (6)

This is a question about meaning and response. Examine how mise-en-scène can communicate ideas to an audience. Remember different audiences can respond to a particular setting in different ways. Aim to make around 3 or 4 detailed points.

(d) Choose a key sequence from your close study film. Explore how one of the following is represented in it – age, gender, ethnicity, social class, disability. (10)

EARLY WARNING ALERT!
Make sure that you refer to a key sequence. Do not talk about the whole film. Don't describe, analyse! You are being assessed on your ability to explore how film language communicates in a short sequence.

This question is worth 10 marks so make sure you give clear, detailed explanations of the ways in which film language is used to represent the social group you have chosen.

Total = 20 marks

Quickfire answers:

Tsotsi

1. Issues of poverty, homelessness and social deprivation are presented. This is shown in the concrete pipes situated on wasteland on the outskirts of the City. It is part of a flashback used in the narrative to tell us more about Tsotsi's childhood. We see the terrible conditions that Tsotsi had to endure as a child and perhaps begin to understand why he has become a criminal. Links are made between the young children still living there years later. The pipes, which should have been used for building houses in a post-apartheid South Africa, are still home to the orphans created by poverty and AIDS.

2. Tsotsi's shack relates to the theme of poverty. It is made from found materials and contains broken electrical items which we assume he has stolen (this could relate to the issue of crime). His shack shows he is poor because it only has one room and no basic facilities like running water. He has a bed but no other home comforts and the place is dark and dirty.

   Miriam's house contrasts with Tsotsi's and even though it too is basic, it is a home. The main difference in their houses is light and colour. Where Tsotsi's shack is dark and contains no windows, Miriam's house is light and feels airy. It is tidy and there seems a place for everything – coloured cotton reels are stacked neatly on a shelf, for example. She obviously takes pride in her home as evidenced by the neatly made bed (compare with Tsotsi's) and her attempt to decorate the place with beautiful mobiles. The light-reflecting glass mobiles are obviously symbolic and it is an important point in the film when the light from the coloured glass plays across Tsotsi's face – he is touched by Miriam's optimistic hope.

3. Fela is a gangster and a successful one at that. Hood conveys this through Fela's costume and props. He is often centrally framed and surrounded by women and cars – symbols of his success. He wears sharp 'zoot' suits and gold jewellery to show off his wealth and status. His suit is purple, which holds the connotations of royalty – indeed, he is like the king of the township. Fela very much stands out amongst the scruffy, aspiring gangsters like Butcher. His suit shows that he is an important businessman (despite his business being questionable) and is to be respected. His body language is confident and powerful and he controls those around him. This implies that the only way to success in the townships is through criminal activity and organised gangs.

4. We quickly identify Tsotsi as a stereotypical thug in the opening sequence of the film. He says little and appears fearless, gesturing to Fela as he walks with his 'gang' through the township. He wears a leather jacket; a hoody shrouds much of his face in the railway station, acting as a disguise. His face is mainly expressionless, and lighting accentuates his hard, unfeeling stare.

The Devil's Backbone

5. The kitchen contains the secret hiding place for Republican gold. Jacinto's actions are largely driven by his desire to find the gold and escape the orphanage. The courtyard encloses the huge rusting bomb. We are told at the beginning of the film that it has been defused but it still ticks, it seems know the secret of Santi's death and in one scene its flag appears to point the way to the basement so that Carlos may also discover the secret.

   The ghost of Casares follows the boys to the orphanage gates at the close of the film. His existence is revealed to the audience but the boys are not aware of his presence as they begin their long journey towards the challenge of living in a fascist-controlled Spain.

6. It is up to you to decide what these mean. There are a number of different interpretations. Does it mean he has always been a ghost and this is his retelling of the story? Is it an ironic comment from a man of science who seemed not to believe in the existence of ghosts? Does it imply that his spirit will guide the boys on their journey to adulthood? Or have you got another theory?

7. Casares calls the liquid 'limbo water'. The term limbo refers to a period of neglect or waiting. The liquid holds in suspension the foetuses of deformed babies. Then there are numerous close-ups of the jars showing the thick amber liquid, full of tiny particles, wrapping itself around the bodies. They perhaps symbolise the generations of children across the world who are physically or emotionally trapped by the horrors of war and will never grow to reach their full potential.

8. The pool serves as a reminder of Jacinto's greed and violence and his guilty secret. There are obvious similarities between the jars and the pool. Both are filled by a thick amber liquid. Both hold bodies 'suspended in time'. Both seem to represent the idea of war 'a tragedy condemned to repeat itself time and again'.

9. The cross-dissolves seem to slow down Jaime's approach to the bomb. Editing combines with lighting to create a ghost-like feel. Dissolves are typically used to suggest a 'cross-over' in terms of meaning. In this case they are used stylistically to highlight Jaime's emotional turmoil at that moment in the past. And, given this is part of a flashback, at the point he retells the story to Carlos. The fact that he touches the bomb underlines its benign nature, at that moment it is the only thing that can offer comfort to Jaime after he has witnessed Santi's death.

10. When we first see Carlos he is travelling in a car towards the orphanage. A number of close-ups show him gazing curiously out of the window. He appears calm, there's a slight smile on his face. This calmness and curiosity is again underlined as he reaches the orphanage when he explores and listens to the bomb. There is a marked contrast between Carlos and the other boys. He is dressed smartly in jacket and trousers; he carries a case and books. His actions are clearly placed centre frame, marking him out as the film's main protagonist.

11. Costume – the white, sleeveless vest emphasising his physicality.

    Facial expression – dark, unblinking eyes, threatening look.

    Smoke coming from his mouth – the devil? This is someone who displays his strength and sexuality, it is his source of power. In binary opposition to Casares who wears a suit and hat whose only source of power is intellectual.

12. Santi is a ghost who has been entombed in the pool. When we see him, particles of the water are suspended around his image. His voice, too, reflects the nature of his entombment.

The Wave

13. Body language is obviously important. Day 1 shows the students slumped in their chairs, drinking from cans, talking, not paying attention. Their clothes also tell us a lot about them. Wenger too doesn't seem too interested, his casual dress, jeans and T-shirt underline a casual attitude towards the project. Day 2 – the body language of teacher and students has changed, Wenger has everyone's attention. Uniforms (white shirts, dark trousers) have replaced designer jeans, leather jackets, baseball caps, etc. Disorder has been replaced by order and a sense of group identity.

14. Mise-en-scène in this sequence underlines his powerful position. An over-the-shoulder shot shows him entering the stage framed by black curtains, he is centre frame and the students are below him, forced to look up to their leader. Low-angle shots then show Wenger centre stage flanked by his 'right-hand men' who appear to act almost as bodyguards. He wears the Wave's uniform. Further over-the-shoulder shots accentuate his thick neck, shaved head and muscular frame. Repeated close-ups, as he becomes more and more 'fired up', show him sweating and spitting as he works himself and his students into a frenzy. He does not blink, his eyes remain fixed upon the students, his expression becomes increasingly manic, his voice louder as he builds to a crescendo. He dominates as the students cheer and applaud.

15. Wenger has his head shaved, there's stubble around his chin. He wears a short-sleeved Ramones T-shirt (the Ramones were a 1970s Punk Rock band) and blue jeans. He is muscular; he looks physically strong and is clearly not intimidated by Weiland. Herr Weiland is a stark contrast to Wenger. He wears a jacket, shirt and tie. He is obviously 'old school'. Wenger's clothes differ very little from those of his students. Weiland's set him apart from them. The appearance of the two men echoes their teaching styles and political views. Wenger is an anarchist; Weiland is very much an establishment figure.

16. Both groups are lined up against each other on opposite sides of the frame. There is a line which appears to divide them. Immediately this gives the impression that once this line is crossed there will be conflict. The body language of the 'black shirts' is aggressive. The white shirts appear to be mocking the other group. Although each group is made up of individuals there is a tendency to judge them by their appearance. Creating a group identity can give individuals a sense of solidarity and belonging. Alternatively it can lead to prejudice – anyone who is perceived as 'different' should be feared or mocked.

Section 5: Controlled Assessment

1: Introduction

The Controlled Assessment is worth 50% of the overall Film Studies GCSE and is your opportunity to investigate existing films in some depth and bring your own creative ideas to realisation. It consists of two main items: a film exploration (two tasks) and a production (four tasks). The key to success in both items is careful research, detailed planning and a willingness to match creativity with technical skills. Before you start your production, do an audit! Note down what skills you have. Are you a keen photographer? Do you love writing? Are you interested in film-making? If so where do your interests lie – camerawork, editing, sound? What equipment is available at school? What do you have at home? When you've done this, look carefully at the options, talk them through with your teacher and begin your research.

2: Exploring film

Researching your film (10 marks)

This element of film exploration is designed to test your research skills together with your understanding of the film industry (production, distribution and exhibition). By now you may have completed this task, if so you can check your work against the guidelines below. If you haven't yet completed it, the guidelines will provide you with advice on selecting research and key questions that should be addressed. Firstly, be clear what is meant by the three important industry terms.

Production, distribution and exhibition details

- Production: who made it and how?
- Distribution: who sold it and how?
- Exhibition: who watched it, where and why?

When choosing a film to research, it's advisable to select a fairly recent one, simply because you will be able to access a lot more relevant information about it, such as the production budget and box office figures, etc. Some students who have chosen obscure films from the 80s, for example, have struggled to find much relevant

Moderator tip

www.boxofficemojo.com is an invaluable site used by the film industry. It details all the latest box office figures daily and compiles really useful lists of films.

information. When carrying out your research look for a range of sources and try to look beyond Wikipedia! There are a lot of very useful websites out there and a bit of searching and sifting beyond the obvious will bring about some interesting and fruitful findings. For example, look at the range of research the candidate below has engaged with in order to give a thorough and focused investigation into their chosen film.

Keep a log of all your research. Even if you find some of it irrelevant, you could still put it in a bibliography to demonstrate the range of research you've undertaken.

Inglourious Basterds (Tarantino, 2009)

Production details

*Inglourious Basterd*s was produced by Universal Pictures, The Weinstein Company and A Band Apart at an estimated production budget of $70,000,000 that was financed by Universal Pictures and The Weinstein Company. It is an American and German film that is in French, German (both with English subtitles) and English. It was produced by Lawrence Bender and written and directed by Quentin Tarantino. It was edited by Sally Menke and the cinematography was done by Robert Richardson. Mary Ramos supervised the music. The film starred Brad Pitt (Lt. Aldo Raine), Christoph Waltz (Col. Hans Landa) and Diane Kruger (Frau Von Hammersmark). Interestingly, the director, Quentin Tarantino, had been working on the script for more than a decade before the film's production.

Budget

Production team

Production companies

Countries of origin

Actors & roles

Distribution details

The theatrical distributor for the film in the UK was Universal Pictures International and in the US was The Weinstein Company. The film is now available on DVD as a one or two disc edition or as a blu-ray disc. On its opening week it sold 1,581,220 DVDs making $28,467,652 and was number two, coming after 2009's comedy *The Hangover*. It was released on DVD on 15 December 2009. Taglines include 'Brad Pitt is a Basterd' and 'A basterd's work is never done'. The film first premiered at the Cannes film festival on 20 May 2009 and won Best Actor (Christoph Waltz) and Quentin Tarantino was nominated for the Palme d'Or award. Oscar-wise *Inglourious Basterds* was nominated for eight academy awards including Best Picture, Best Director and Best Supporting Actor, which was its only Oscar win.

Distribution in cinema & DVD release

Screening details

Nominations & awards

Exhibition details

Inglourious Basterds was released on 21st August 2009 and stopped screening in the UK on 24 September 2009. In the UK it grossed $16,439,434 in total and in the US it has made $120,540,719 but outside America it has made $200,914,970 meaning worldwide it has made $321,455,689. It is rated an 18 in the UK and Ireland and an R in the US. It is Tarantino's highest

Box office takings

Certification

grossing both in America and Worldwide to date. It mostly received positive reviews with a score of 8.4 out of 10 on IMDB and 88% at Rotten Tomatoes. Empire magazine described it as '*With a confidence typical of its director, the last line of* Inglourious Basterds *is, "This might just be my masterpiece". While that may not be true, this is an often dazzling movie that sees QT back on exhilarating form.*' However, unsurprisingly the film encountered controversy about the title of the film but surprisingly more controversy was encountered about the spelling of 'inglourious' rather than the latter part of the title. The film also encountered controversy because Universal Pictures (the production company) had to censor the German publicity site for the film as on the website and throughout the film swastikas feature prominently and this is obviously prohibited in Germany so was consequently removed from the website.

I used the following websites to gather information:

www.imdb.com, www.rottentomatoes.com, www.boxofficemojo.com, www.empireonline.com & www.theguardian.co.uk

Interesting & relevant facts about release →

Critical reviews from respected sources →

Censorship →

A range of sources cited →

Moderator feedback

This is a confident, detailed and carefully researched piece. The candidate demonstrates excellent knowledge and understanding of the three key areas of the film industry and uses well-integrated specialist terminology. A Level 4 response.

Micro analysis of a film sequence (20 marks)

This section of the Controlled Assessment gives you the opportunity to extend your initial research into the film of your choice and consider the ways in which meanings are created in a short sequence of that film.

You should focus on **two** micro aspects of your chosen sequence, explaining how meaning is created and how an audience might respond:

- Cinematography
- Editing
- Sound
- Mise-en-scène.

Moderator tip

Don't simply describe what you see/hear because anyone can do that. You should use your film language knowledge to describe a sound layer (for example), and then explain what effect it has on the audience.

Your choice of film is very important here. Choose an interesting extract, one which gives you lots to say in terms of how two elements of film language communicate to an audience. Sometimes the sequences you like best don't allow you to really demonstrate knowledge and understanding together with your grasp of terminology. Some genres, for example comedy, can prove very challenging to analyse. You only need to analyse about 3 minutes' worth of footage but make sure you have lots to write about it. Choose your focus to fit the extract – if you've chosen sound then make sure there are a lot of different sound techniques used to create certain effects.

REMEMBER: Superhero films or those on the Films Outside Hollywood list for Paper 2 must not be used for the Film Research component.

The student that submitted the research on *Inglourious Basterds* is called Leo. Let's look at an extract from his micro analysis:

Annotation boxes (left margin)

Title – Film and which 2 micro elements, Leo clearly states his focus.

Focus is on the movement of the camera. The sequence has been stopped almost frame by frame so Leo is able to explain how the pace of the sequence has been created through editing.

Audience response is acknowledged.

Camera shot types and their purpose are identified.

Pace of editing is explained.

Understands how length of shot affects the pace of the piece.
The camera's lack of movement is also identified.

The frequent description of camera angle, height **and** effect demonstrates a confident technical knowledge.

Leo is able to recognise how directors 'borrow' from each other. His understanding of this homage helps him to stand out as a real film enthusiast.

Micro Analysis of a film sequence – The cinematography and editing used in 'Nation's Pride' (Dir: Eli Roth) from the film '*Inglourious Basterds*' (Dir: Quentin Tarantino, 2009).

In terms of the cinematography of the film, mostly **static camera shots** are used with few **camera pans or tracking shots**. This is because most of the shots used in the film are only a couple of seconds long at best and some only a split second long, so the fast **pace** of the film comes from the **quick cut edits** and most of the movement is from the editing rather than the action.

The film begins with a **static mid-shot** of the protagonist, Frederick Zoller (Daniel Bruhl) looking determined, confident and serious dressed in Nazi uniform with his helmet on and his rifle ready. We see him look at something but we the audience do not see what he sees, so far giving the film a restricted narrative. The camera then **cuts to a long shot** of an alley-way where a truck pulls up and American soldiers disembark and sprint off. This shot establishes the location – an old rural village in Italy which is emphasised by the cobbled roads and archways. There then follows a succession of **quick cut edits which rapidly cut** between Zoller at the top of an impenetrable tower and his enemies below.

… From here, the **pace** becomes slower because most of the shots become longer. We now get a **static long shot** of the first civilian we have seen – a mother pushing her baby in a pram. Unfortunately, in his rush to get to cover, a clumsy soldier runs past and knocks the pram away from her. A **high-angle POV** from Zoller sees the pram look vulnerable rolling along amongst all the death and destruction. This is followed by a **medium low angle tracking shot** that tracks the wheels of the pram rolling down the hill. This **cuts to a tight close up** of the distraught mother shouting 'Mio Bambino!' The camera returns to the low tracking shot facing the wheels. An **eye level shot** sees a soldier run up to the pram, then the **camera pans** as he hoists the baby up to shield himself from Zoller. The **camera cuts to a close up** of Zoller who lowers his rifle and looks horrified. The **camera reverses to a high angle shot** where the soldier sprints across the square using the crying baby for cover then he tosses the baby into the mother's arms. This scene is an homage to *Battleship Potemkin* (1925, dir: Sergei Eisenstein), a stylised Russian film about revolution. In a famous scene, a mother is shot and her pram rolls away down the Odessa Steps…

Note: Schools and Colleges are responsible for overseeing the students' individual choice of film for the analysis of micro elements in a film sequence.

Moderator feedback

This is a sophisticated Level 4 response to a challenging sequence. An excellent ability to explore micro elements of the film sequence is demonstrated here as the candidate consistently identifies specific camera shots using appropriate film terminology. How meanings are created and responses are evoked is at the forefront of this analysis.

Clearly Leo has spent quite a lot of time focusing on the ways in which cinematography and editing create meaning and response in his sequence. This has involved playing the sequence over several times using the pause button to identify and time shots. He has also incorporated knowledge and understanding of editing gained during other areas of his studies. Film language has been accurately identified and possible meanings interrogated. The final piece has benefitted from the redrafting process. Make sure you do the same, don't just submit the first draft of your micro analysis. Seek advice from your teacher/peers about how to improve. Read each other's work and check to see if the focus (on cinematography, editing, sound or mise en scène) is clear.

Checklist: ask why?

Have you used your knowledge of film language to good effect here? Have you explained:

- Camera shot types (distance and angle) and why
- Camera movement and why
- Lighting and why
- Editing – what kind of transitions and why.

Remember – always ask 'why'.

3: Pitching your film

Pitching your film (10 marks)

It is important to consider all your options in terms of pre-production and production work before creating your pitch. Decide which genre of film you are going to be selling, think about the advantages and disadvantages of particular kinds of narratives. If you really want to create a film sequence for your final production, how problematic could it be if you pitch an idea for a sci-fi film along the lines of Alfonso Cuaron's latest release *Gravity*? You may find it useful to outline a structure for pre-production and production work. Here is Leo's:

Pitch – War Game – an 'homage' to *Platoon, Apocalypse Now* and *Saving Private Ryan*.

Pre-production – storyboard – use photos for short fight sequence. Location: woods near my house. Props: camouflage suits, replica guns.

Production – short film using storyboard ideas – make notes on editing and camerawork for evaluative analysis.

The pitch is your opportunity to **sell** your film idea to potential investors and cinema audiences. You are pitching an idea for a film that has not been made yet and the purpose of the pitch is to get investors on board. What is being assessed here is your ability to propose plausible ideas for new films and demonstrate an understanding of the film industry and its audiences.

Pitch

Your logline should be concise and encapsulate the essence of your film in one sentence.

In Leo's logline below he manages to summarise the plot, establish the genre and set up an enigma which would (hopefully) intrigue the studio and get him a meeting with potential backers.

PITCH FOR WAR GAME

Logline = A group of four young friends who share an obsession with war films take their games too far and end up on the battlefield in a conflict where the games become all too real.

'War Game' is a hybrid combining a coming of age film and a war film. It explores a young boy's journey from innocence to experience and pays homage to classic modern war films such as 'Platoon' and 'Apocalypse Now'. However, the main inspiration comes from 'Son of Rambow' with its focus on a young boy's experience and obsession with war and its light-hearted 'buddy' feel.

The target audience is mostly male with a primary focus on teens 12–19 (reflected in the characters). A secondary audience of adults would appreciate/understand the homages to other war films. The cast would be mostly non-professional but Paddy Considine (usually associated with low budget British films) could play the boys' mentor, creating a convincing, sympathetic role model.

The narrative revolves around the friendship of four young schoolboys. It begins with a light-hearted look at their obsession with war but becomes much darker as this spirals out of control when the youngest lies about his age and signs up to fight in a Middle Eastern conflict. The friends are then drawn deeper and deeper into the horrors of war. Their games become a nightmare reality and innocence is shattered. The narrative follows a cyclical structure, beginning at the end and leaving the audience not knowing if the protagonist lives or dies.

Moderator feedback

This candidate creates an effective logline and identifies the film's genre and similar films. He offers an interesting and 'bankable' idea and demonstrates a good understanding of film audiences and industry. Indeed, he gives a thoughtful consideration of his audience and shows how he will capture their interest through appropriate casting and production.

4: Choosing and creating a pre-production option

Pre-production (20 marks)

The pre-production options can be broadly separated into two categories: those which emerge from the study of film language, genre and narrative (screenplay and storyboards) and those emerging from the study of film industries (merchandising campaign and magazine cover/contents). Whichever option you chose it **must** link to the idea you have outlined in your pitch.

Screenplay

One pre-production option you could create is an extract from a screenplay. It is important that you show understanding of how screenplays are set out (their format). Having a framework will help you to think in cinematic terms. Below is your checklist. If you have already completed your screenplay, go through it and check you have included all of the following. If you haven't started yet, make sure you use these when you set out your screenplay:

- **Scene** – screenplays are divided into scenes. Each scene covers dramatic action taking place at a particular place at a specific time.
- **Slug line** – the scene heading which indicates whether the action takes place inside or outside, where it is and what part of the day it is.
- **Scene direction** – this refers to the action, what the audience will see when they are watching the film.
- **Character heading** – name of the character who is about to speak (usually CAPITALISED and centred above the dialogue).
- **Dialogue** – what the characters say.

Remember, a screenplay creates for an audio-visual medium. Films can be both seen and heard but it is predominantly the visual action that drives the narrative forward. Seeing a character do something is usually far more powerful than listening to them talking about it.

Look at the extract from the screenplay that follows and note how the candidate concentrates mostly on cinematic storytelling rather than dialogue. The description of action, movement and mise-en-scène really help us to visualise this candidate's idea.

Key terms

Slug line
The scene heading which indicates whether the action takes place inside or outside, where it is and what part of the day it is.

Scene directions
The action, what is seen on the screen.

Character heading
The name of the character in a film script who is about to speak (usually capitalised and centred above the dialogue).

Dialogue
What the characters say.

Moderator tip

The BBC Writer's Room is another invaluable resource which will help you present your screenplay in an appropriate and professional way: **www.bbc.co.uk/ writersroom**

Moderator tip

If you have already completed your screenplay, check to see how much dialogue you have included. If the **dialogue** outweighs the **scene directions**, you have probably ignored the importance of what is seen on the screen.

Section 5
4: Choosing and creating a
pre-production option

SCREENPLAY FOR ZOMBIE SCHOOL

SCENE 2

FADE IN:

INT. SCHOOL CORRIDOR - NIGHT

THREE TEENAGE BOYS ARE RUNNING ALONG AN UNLIT SCHOOL CORRIDOR, TRYING EACH DOOR AS THEY COME TO IT. ALL ARE LOCKED. THEY ARE PANTING FOR BREATH AND OBVIOUSLY FRIGHTENED.

LEWIS

I don't believe it! All of them, locked!

TAL

What are we going to do? They'll see us here easily.

JORDAN

We could smash the glass and hide under the benches.

LEWIS

They'll see the glass!

JORDAN

Well, we can't go back that way, can we?

TAL

Oh, God, this isn't funny now.

(DISTANT SOUNDS OF RUNNING FOOTSTEPS MAKE THE BOYS TURN AND PEER DOWN THE DIM CORRIDOR. THEY START PANICKING AND JORDAN PUNCHES THE GLASS DOOR WHICH SPLINTERS.)

LEWIS

Hurry!

(JORDAN WRAPS HIS HOODIE ROUND HIS FIST AND BREAKS THE SPLINTERED GLASS. HE CLIMBS THROUGH AND BECKONS FOR THE OTHERS TO FOLLOW HIM. THE RISING SOUND OF FOOTSTEPS IS ACCOMPANIED BY LOW MOANING BUT AS YET, THE CORRIDOR IS DARK AND STILL EMPTY. INSIDE THE CLASSROOM, THE BOYS COWER UNDER A DESK AT THE BACK. ABOVE THEM IS A POSTER WHICH READS 'KEEP CALM AND CARRY ON'.

(SUDDENLY, OUT OF THE GLOOM A FIGURE LURCHES FORWARD AND THEN STOPS. IT SEEMS TO SNIFF THE AIR AND PAUSE TO LISTEN. IT MOVES INTO THE LIGHT AND WE SEE IT IS A ZOMBIE. IT SHUFFLES FORWARD AND TRIES THE HANDLE OF THE DOOR, FORCES OPEN THE LOCK AND STANDS FRAMED IN THE DOORWAY. ONE OF THE BOYS EMITS A SMALL SCREAM. THE ZOMBIE THROWS ITS HEAD BACK AND RELEASES A LONG, LOW MOAN...)

A cliffhanger device is used to 'hook' the audience

The slug line introduces the scene and indicates whether the location is INT = Interior or Ext = Exterior

Screen directions (what is seen on screen) are always written in the present tense. This is not a shooting script, so camera directions, etc., aren't necessary

Conflict and action are established immediately making for an arresting opening

Enigma codes are used to get the audience asking questions:
Why are they in school at night?
What are they running from?
Why are they scared?
What will happen next?

Scene directions are in bold capitals and dialogue in lower case and centred
Font is Courier and usually size 12

Genre is obvious through the range of recognisable conventions used

Moderator feedback

This response demonstrates excellent planning and presentational skills. The candidate follows appropriate screenplay conventions to good effect. Dialogue and screen directions are well balanced and generic conventions are used creatively and applied with confidence.

Storyboard

This is the perfect option if you want to go on and make a short film sequence for your final production. Storyboards are vital planning tools. Most mainstream films will be storyboarded before filming begins. Don't underestimate their importance. They really help you to visualise and sequence your narrative. Unless you are a fantastic artist, we would recommend you use a digital camera to take photos for your storyboard. You can create your own template, or your teacher might have one for you to use. You should aim for approximately 20 frames and again an awareness of appropriate format is vital if you are to reach the higher levels for your work.

Let's look at Leo's planning storyboard as an example. Although there are only two frames, a fairly clear idea of genre is already indicated. Shots are accurately identified with believable timings and appropriate transitions. A sophisticated understanding of shot levels is also demonstrated alongside a careful consideration of the ways in which sound creates meaning. All this and more in two frames! Leo produced 23 frames which then created the solid framework for a film sequence and you could do the same! Try to visualise and account for every second of the sequence. Aim for a variety of shot lengths. Remember not every shot is 3 seconds!

> *Moderator tip*
>
> Begin your pre-production work with some careful research. Look on the Internet to view professional storyboards. Don't draw your storyboard unless, like Guillermo Del Toro, you are an amazing artist. Mise-en-scène is important; stick men on a white background do little to evidence an excellent understanding of genre and narrative.

Frame number

Explanation of what is in the frame – where it is set, what is happening, how it is lit, etc…

What kind of camera angle is used, how long the shot lasts, how this frame moves to the next…

SHOT	FRAME	ACTION	CAMERA	SOUND
19		Exterior Daylight Thick woodland Protagonist aims at boy 3 in close distance	POV shot of protagonist looking down the barrel of his gun to boy 3 2 seconds Quick cut edit to…	Diegetic: Toy gun shots Distant shouts Non-diegetic track: John Murphy's 'In the house – in a heartbeat'
SHOT	FRAME	ACTION	CAMERA	SOUND
20		Exterior Daylight Thick woodland Boy 3 aims at protagonist in close distance	Reverse POV shot of boy 3 looking down the barrel of his gun to protagonist 2 seconds Quick cut edit to…	Diegetic: Toy gun shots Distant shouts Non-diegetic track: John Murphy's 'In the house – in a heartbeat'

The still camera acts as the dv camera in terms of height, distance and angle

Sound is specified in terms of diegetic (that is part of the film world) and non-diegetic (that is added in post-production to create certain effects)

Below is a checklist. If you have already completed your storyboard, go through it and check you have included all of the following. If you haven't started yet, make sure you use these when you set out your storyboard:

- **Frame number** – this relates to where in the film a particular shot will be.
- **Shot description** – camera angle, distance and any movement.
- **Action** – a brief written description of action taking place in the shot.
- **Shot duration** – how long a shot lasts (typically from 1 to 5 seconds).
- **Sound** – may include dialogue, music, sound effects, ambient noise.
- **Edit type** – the kind of transition that is used when moving from one shot to another, e.g. straight cut, dissolve, fade.

Marketing campaign

The process of marketing a film begins very early in its life, often before filming has even begun. This option offers lots of possibilities but again research is key. Make sure you are clear about the part your products play within an overall campaign and make sure you demonstrate a creative awareness of the codes and conventions used.

One poster isn't a marketing campaign! The specification requires you to produce at least four items. If you are aiming for the higher levels, they should show a creative understanding of a range of products which would be used to market (promote, raise awareness, sell) your film. This might include front of house materials for the cinema (standees), plans for viral marketing 'stunts' or customised packaging for food stuffs featuring your own film artwork/central character. Below is a checklist. If you have already completed your marketing campaign, go through it and check you have included a variety of products. If you haven't started yet, you may want to use some of these suggestions:

- **Teaser poster** – a poster that is different from those used when the film is about to be released. Most consist of a strong central image, a **tagline** and a vague indication of when it may be released, e.g. 'Coming soon' 'This Xmas'.
- **Display items for cinema foyer** – large cardboard 'cut outs' which are often three-dimensional and are designed to stand in cinema foyers.
- **Viral adverts** – ads that do not necessarily give away the identity of a film but are designed to get people surfing the Internet in order to discover more about it.
- **Merchandise** – products such as action figures linked to the film and intended for sale.
- **Tie-in products** – often special edition versions of existing products, e.g. Happy Meal boxes at McDonalds.
- **Screen saver/wallpaper** – images from the film's artwork that can be downloaded onto your computer or mobile phone.

Key term

Tagline
A memorable phrase that sums up a film, e.g. *Jaws* 'Just when you thought it was safe to go back in the water'.

Look at how inventive some existing film marketing campaigns have been:

An authentic-looking Missing poster which featured the fictional characters from *The Blair Witch Project* (1999)

Public warning signs pasted on benches, bus-stops and vehicles alerted audiences to themes in the 2009 film, *District 9*

A character from the film, *Prometheus* (2012) gives a pretend TED talk from the future in 2023. It could be viewed on the fictitious Weyland Industries website (another marketing stunt).

Key term

Mode of address
The tone or written style of a magazine article. How it talks to or appeals to its audience.

Magazine cover and contents page

This option again requires careful research. Your front cover and contents should be for a **new** film magazine, so don't call it *Empire* or *Total Film*! It must be produced digitally so you cannot draw it by hand. You don't have to use original images but it's great if you do as it helps to evidence both creativity and strong presentational skills. Make sure you have studied other film magazines closely (*Empire*, *Total Film*, *Sight and Sound*) so you are able to emulate their language, style, tone and **mode of address.**

The cover

This option has **two** parts, a front page and a contents page. Each of these parts typically uses slightly different codes and conventions because they fulfil different purposes. The front cover is designed to attract the buyer.

Total Film Magazine: The big sell? Only one main image.

Below is a checklist for the cover. If you have already completed your magazine cover, go through it and check you have used the appropriate codes and conventions. If you haven't started yet, make sure you pay close attention to them:

- **Masthead** – this contains the name you have chosen for your magazine. Typically it is placed near the top of the page and is big and bold so it stands out from its competitors.

- **Strapline** – situated at the top of the page just above the masthead, designed to make the reader want to open the magazine and read on.

- **Cover lines** – the main cover line is often situated directly below the masthead. Other cover lines, often called 'puffs', are typically placed at the sides of the cover. They tell us what articles are in the magazine.

- **Central image** – a large image designed to stand out, often features one star who looks straight out at the audience.

- **House style** – you should also think about the style of your magazine. Different film magazines use different house styles – particular uses of colour, font style, layout and design that help an audience to identify their product.

When the emphasis is on one main film a front cover will be stripped of 'puffs' in order to underline the importance of the film and acknowledge its 'pulling power' in terms of attracting fans and other existing audiences. This technique may be useful for you as the specification requires your **new** magazine to sell your **new** film (the film you have outlined in your pitch). Of course you don't have access to 'real-life' stars to use for your central image but with a little imagination, a few props (ask the drama department) and a willing friend or family member; you can recreate a very effective, unique cover.

Key terms

Masthead
This contains the name of a magazine. Typically it is placed near the top of the page and is big and bold so it stands out from its competitors.

Strapline
Situated at the top of the page just above the masthead, designed to make the reader want to open the magazine and read on.

Cover lines
The main cover line is often situated directly below the masthead. Other cover lines, often called 'puffs', are typically placed at the sides of the cover. They tell us what articles are in the magazine.

Central image
A large image designed to stand out, often features one star who looks straight out at the audience.

House style
You should also think about the style of your magazine. Different film magazines use different house styles – particular uses of colour, font style, layout and design that help an audience to identify their product.

Moderator tip

Make sure you create your own 'house style' when designing your magazine cover – check that this 'house style' is still clearly evidenced in your contents page.

CONTENTS — Contents title: Usually in bold black against white background.

Miniature version of front cover. Page numbers with article title and taglines.

House style still evidenced.

Different logos which indicate different focus sections of magazines.

Middle column larger than two side columns; central dominating image.

Focus sections to attract different interest groups.

Contents page

The contents page is designed to help the audience navigate its way through the magazine after purchase. Below is your checklist of appropriate conventions:

- The house style of your magazine should be evident although the layout will be quite different from the front cover. ✓

- A white background with black font is often incorporated in order to make contents easy to read. ✓

- It should be organised and structured in order to make the magazine easier to read for its audience. ✓

- The contents should be clearly indicated in page order but not all pages are included, just a selection chosen in order to appeal to the audience. ✓

- Smaller versions of images contained on the front page may be incorporated. ✓

- Advertisements may be included, selected in order to appeal to the magazine's audience. ✓

The contents page above demonstrates the differences and similarities required in terms of style, codes and conventions.

Section 5
5: Choosing and creating
a production option

5: Choosing and creating a production option

Production (35 marks)

You may have already chosen which of the production options most suits your talents and enthusiasm. All of the options should follow-on from your pitch and pre-production work. There is, however, one exception. If you have decided to create your own film sequence, you can work with others, providing there are no more than four of you in the group. With this option each of you must take responsibility for a specific role in the film-making process. All of the options together with advice on how you can create as professional a film product as possible are considered in this section.

Poster campaign

Posters are an important marketing technique. They attract new audiences and entice existing fans.

You should produce **at least three** different posters that form part of a cohesive campaign. You could create a **teaser poster campaign**. This offers the audience a limited amount of information but gets them thinking about what the poster might be for. Several linked posters are released gradually running up to the release of the film. The prospective audience is 'teased' by puzzles or questions (enigmas) which withhold information about the film. Often the teaser posters progressively add more detail as the film nears release, giving further information about stars/director/release date, etc. You may want to create a **main theatrical poster.** This poster typically contains much more information, e.g. production team, distributor, stars, release date.

As with all your creative work, research is key, you must have a clear idea what is meant by a poster campaign and be able show a confident grasp of the conventions typically used in the posters that make up that campaign. Posters may have different USPs (unique selling points), these could be stars, they could be iconic images, e.g. Batman's logo.

No matter what campaign you choose to create you MUST ALSO USE ORIGINAL IMAGES. This is not nearly as daunting as it sounds! Look at these four posters for *Contagion*, they basically just use six images, close-ups and extreme close-ups taken from slightly different angles. Tom Cruise may be busy if you have chosen him for the lead in your action film but that doesn't stop you searching for posters with him on them, strong-arming a friend, or relative, and replicating body language, camera shots and costume for your poster. You could work with a range of related images or characters – have a look at the poster campaign shown

here. *Contagion* (2011) is an **ensemble-led** film; a different poster has been created for each star/character whilst maintaining the same colour scheme/font/layout to maintain its brand image.

Before starting your works you should have looked at a range of posters, analysed the conventions used, and identified where and when they would be displayed.

Below is a checklist of the main conventions used when creating a poster campaign:

- **Tagline** – 'nothing spreads like fear' see *Contagion* above.
- **Critics' quotes** – short positive quotes taken from longer reviews written by film critics. '*Gravity* is a masterpiece of cinematography, technical direction, and storytelling all at once.'
- **5 Star ratings** – usually taken from film, Internet or newspaper reviews.
- **Comparisons with other films** – '*Gravity* is the 21st century's answer to *2001 A Space Odyssey*'
- **Hook** – what draws the audience in, it may be an image, tagline or star.
- **Star billing** – where the stars' names or images are positioned on the poster, often indicating their importance in terms of selling power.
- **Iconography** – props, setting, costumes, which signal the genre of the film.
- **Genre** – use generic conventions/iconography.
- **Narrative** – clues (visual or language based) which communicate some idea of what the film is about.

Film sequence

This option is a great way to demonstrate your knowledge and understanding of film language. Again research is important; make sure you have viewed several short film sequences (YouTube a useful source). Pick two short sequences that are approximately 90 seconds long and make notes on each. Using the pause button, note down the types of shots used, timings and editing. You should also think about the ways in which sound is used and genre is signalled.

So your first checklist should consist of the following 'micro' elements:

- Cinematography to include the types of shot, angles used, camera movement. You should also consider mise-en-scène. How shots are framed and what they contain.
- Editing – to include the speed of editing and the types of transitions used.
- Sound – to include dialogue, sound effects, background music, ambient sound.

If you have already made, or are planning to make, a film on your own, you may talk about all of the above in your evaluative analysis. However, you could pick just one element and examine it in some depth if you prefer.

If you have worked or are working in a group of two, each of you should take responsibility for one of the following roles: camerawork, editing or sound design. Of course, in practice, you may have worked collaboratively but your evaluative analysis and your notes made whilst planning and filming should concentrate on your chosen role.

Key terms

Ensemble led
When a group of big stars are used as the USP (unique selling point) for a film.

Star ratings
Usually 5 stars indicating how highly a film has been critically rated.

Hook
The method used to attract an audience.

Moderator tip

When you have completed your poster campaign, lay out each of your posters side-by-side. Are they clearly linked in terms of style and mode of address? Do they contain the necessary conventions?

Moderator tip

Directing, costume design or performing are not appropriate roles to focus on – you must pick at least one of the three 'micro' elements of film language listed. Go back to the film language section of this guide to ensure you correctly identify elements of film language.

Section 5
5: Choosing and creating
a production option

If you are in a group of three or four, it is suggested that two of you should share the responsibility for editing. This is because editing is the most time-consuming and arguably the most challenging role. Make your own notes whilst working so each of you has a different 'take' on the editing process.

Note, you are **not** creating a film trailer, you are applying the skills you learnt from your micro-analysis so we are expecting to see a continuous sequence that uses a range of camera angles and movement, editing and sound to good effect.

A good sequence will make the genre clear and use a variety of techniques to create tension and/or atmosphere. The sequence can be from any part of your film, so obviously choose to create an extract that has some action not just static dialogue which might not be very tense or atmospheric!

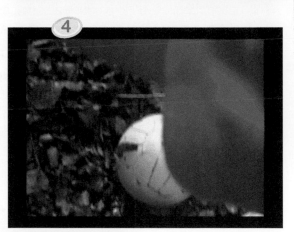

Moderator tip

When the moderator watches your film they may notice that, for example, the cinematography is clearly a high Level 4 but the sound is much weaker. If your role has not been identified on the film credits and in your evaluative analysis, the moderator will find it difficult to determine which level you have reached.

Moderator tip

Always use a tripod unless hand-held shots are absolutely necessary in terms of making meaning. It is tempting to 'excuse' shaky hand-held by stating you aimed to recreate *The Blair Witch Project* but you will almost certainly struggle to demonstrate a range of shots and their meanings if you opt for this technique.

Moderator tip

If you are responsible for sound do not simply download a music track. Instead use a range of sound effects, ambient sound and music. Don't forget that silence creates meaning too!

Pictured are five screen captures from the climactic sequences of Jack's short horror film *Header*. Jack opted to make the film on his own and to evaluate cinematography. By analysing just five of his frames we can clearly see how he manages to demonstrate excellent creative and technical skills.

- Frame 1 is a low level shot showing the searcher's feet as he runs through the woods.

- Frame 2 is a low-angled mid shot showing the searcher's progress. The face of the searcher is not shown; the action and setting are typical of the horror genre.

- The framing in shot 3 has narrative importance, box and football are situated towards the front of the frame, and they may be linked in terms of meaning in some way. Both are white and stand out against the greens and brown of the woodland environment.

- Shot 4, a high-angle close-up, also shows the ability to manipulate focus, the searcher's arm is blurred as he lifts the lid of the box but the football is important, it's in sharp focus.

- Shot 5 is in sharp focus, the high-angle close-up creates an interesting effect. The searcher's feet are resting on the head as if it is a ball about to be kicked. The ball rests on the head as if it is just about to be 'headed' into a goal!

Just five shots, carefully planned, create a high level of meaning and response and lots to write about in an evaluative analysis.

Homepage for website

This option requires you to produce a homepage and at least one linked page promoting your new film. You must use **original images**.

This medium encourages the audience to connect with the text, so will offer quizzes, competitions, downloads, etc. As with every production option, you should begin with research. Look at a number of different websites – it may be useful to you try to find similar genre films to your own. Focus carefully on content and conventions. Examine the kinds of images used, the artwork and style. Below is a checklist of typical contents and conventions:

- URL – the web address for an official website, e.g. www.warmbodiesmovie.com

- Logo – usually on each page of website.

- Gallery – production stills, publicity photographs of stars/actors, images from the film.

- Characters – bios/profiles of major characters.

- Games/competitions – based on characters/narrative of film.

- Downloads – e.g. wallpaper for computers, ring tones for mobiles.

Make sure your website is consistent in terms of style and that it uses more than one repeated image from your film. The specification requires a **minimum** of two pages. Aim to produce enough to demonstrate good creative and technical skills and evidence a clear understanding of how the website helps to market your film.

The example below of the 2013 film 'Warm Bodies' enables its users to watch exclusive video clips, meet characters and use social media links to tweet/blog about their response to the film. As with other marketing methods, the website will have a strong brand image which will come from the choice of consistent fonts, colour schemes and overall style.

Plot synopsis, character profiles, actors' bios, a gallery of images, etc., are all conventions of a film's website.

Users can watch videos, buy tickets, play games/quizzes, share content with friends, etc.

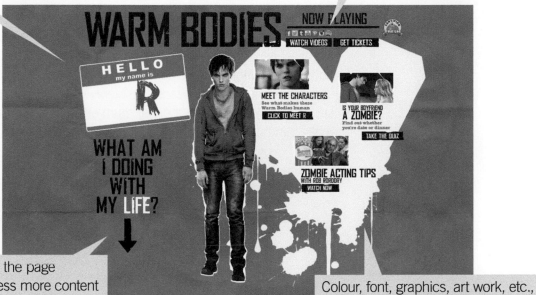

Rolling over graphics on the page enables the user to access more content which is accompanied by a voice-over from the central character.

Colour, font, graphics, art work, etc., is consistent across the marketing mix – posters, trailers and all other promotional materials.

Magazine feature

This option requires you to create a feature based on the production of your new film. The feature can be written for a film, or school/college magazine. It should include star or director interviews, be a minimum of two pages long and contain at least two promotional still photographs. THESE IMAGES MUST BE ORIGINAL.

You will need to emulate the presentation style and mode of address of existing film or school/college magazines. These will have differing house styles and target audiences so be sure to be clear which kind of magazine you are creating. If you look back at the pre-production section that focuses on magazine cover and contents page, you will find some useful hints on content and creating a house style.

When researching the kinds of articles that typically feature in film magazines you may have noticed the close relationship between the film and magazine industries. Magazines are a vitally important way of informing audiences and raising interest in a new film. Below is a checklist of the areas you should consider when creating your magazine articles:

- House style – the style of your magazine. Different film magazines use different house styles – particular uses of colour, font style, layout and design that help an audience to identify their product.

Moderator tip

Avoid downloading interviews with existing stars or directors as this does not allow you to show your creativity, your knowledge and understanding of film language, audiences and film industry.

- Mode of address – the tone or written style of the article. How it addresses its audience.

- Publicity stills – stills distributed to the media by the production marketing team. Usually a mix of 'the making of' stills, 'staged' stills and stills from the film.

- Positivity – interviews, bios, etc., are usually a result of collaboration between the film marketing team and the magazine. Both have a mutual interest in promoting the film so articles are invariably positive.

- Interview, profile, in-production report, reviews – each uses a different style; make sure you are clear which kind of article you are producing.

Below is an example from Leo's press pack (see next section). It is a small part of an interview with the director of his film War Game. You can clearly see how this interview could form the basis of a magazine feature once more photographs are added and adaptations were made in terms of house style and mode of address. The publicity still which 'heads' the interview from War Game is carefully 'staged' to suggest genre and create the maximum effect – note how a simple coloured poster of a flag can be manipulated to look like the real thing.

Interview with Leo Dearden: Director of War Game

So, Leo, where did you get your idea for War Game from?

Well, I feel like I've grown up to a backdrop of stories about men who have gone off to fight for their country with disastrous consequences. I've always loved the genre and felt I had something to add.

Was finding the right location important, given your very limited budget?

We just sort of improvised with what we had and luckily we lived in an ideal rural location for most of the film, like when they're playing in the woods, I mean that's filmed just up my road! I wanted to have a sort of 'Nam' feel to the exterior shots and the oppressive woods felt disorientating and just right.

The soundtrack in War Game is very effective – how did you come to choose those tracks?

Well during the conception of War Game I had been watching *Apocalypse Now* and loved Coppola's use of 'The End' by The Doors at the start so when you hear that in War Game that's just a little homage. Also, I just really liked The Doors at the time (laughs). 'In the House in a Heartbeat' by John Murphy I discovered through 28 Days Later and was thinking about this scene in the film and thought I needed something fast, loud, exciting and slightly sinister so I thought let's try using this. I'm really pleased how that song worked in the film, it had the exact unnerving effect I wanted to create.

Notice how Leo takes the opportunity to demonstrate his knowledge and understanding in this short extract. He mixes the director's personal motivations with a consideration of genre and the importance of setting. His new film takes 'centre stage', the interview is important in terms of the success of his film. He refers to his influences in terms of other films and the ways in which sound can create meaning.

Press pack

One option you could choose to create is a press pack for your new film. This is a terrific option if you have strong writing skills. You have to produce a range of promotional materials to sell the film. These could include: a synopsis, interviews with the director and actors, cast biographies, stills from the film, quotations from critics, etc. Press packs are created in order to allow newspapers, magazines, TV and the Internet 'insider information' ahead of a film's release. This information, developed by the film's marketing team, may then be turned into a news item, critical review or magazine article (see magazine article option in the previous section).

Press packs for new films can be found online but let's look at excerpts from Leo's press pack for War Game below.

Moderator tip
Make sure that you create at least two articles which each have a different focus. Include original images of stars, director or screenwriters and incorporate at least one still from your film. Remember the film and the making of the film must take 'centre stage'.

PRESS RELEASE

War Game heralds the emergence of an exciting new, young British Director. Critics have already created a 'buzz' about his debut film War Game after the first wave of reviews and private viewings this month. War Game is due for release late July and is sure to be a strong contender for the best small budget British film of the year.

War Game follows the story of four friends who share a passion for everything war; loving nothing better than re-enacting favourite bits from classic war films. However, these war games become all too real when one friend lies about his age and joins up to avenge his squaddie brother's death in the Middle East. The others subsequently follow but soon realise that war is not a game.

The Independent has praised War Game for its '*tightly paced, economical script*' and for its central performances, '*the small group of talented actors allow newcomer Dearden to really make an impact with this sensitive subject matter*'. *Total Film* has also been lavish in its praise stating, '*This is what good British cinema is all about – clever dialogue, well-paced action and a universal message that speaks to those on both sides of the conflict*'.

Moderator tip
Make sure you use original, not found, images in your production.

This excerpt from Leo's press release draws attention to storyline, background to production and critical reception. It successfully draws the journalists' attention to the areas they could be exploring when writing about the film.

Below is a checklist of the areas you should consider when creating your press pack:

- Cover page – film title, director, artwork from the film, website, and production company.
- Press release – key details of film including brief synopsis, stars, production background.
- Production stills – images from the film that can be reproduced by the press.
- Bios – brief biographies of key personnel involved in the making of the film.
- Critical reception – positive extracts from critical reviews of the film.
- Star/ director interviews – referring mainly to the film but may also include references to their other work.

Moderator tip

If you are writing bios or interviews don't download existing ones from the Internet. Create your own and demonstrate your creativity and knowledge and understanding of film language.

Production stills

These should be images from the film that can be reproduced by the press. They should include key images which show part of the story accompanied by captions which explain what is going on. Mise-en-scène is important, bear in mind these stills are carefully staged by the production company in order to publicise/sell their film.

Director Leo Dearden's 'homage' to Platoon

War Game 2013: The three friends leave their war games behind

A new discovery? Dearden checks the rushes for War Game

Let's look again at a small selection of Leo's stills.

Three original images which convey a fair amount of information: the first still is taken from the film and clearly shows the influences talked about in the press release, the second conveys a little of the story and the third expands information given about the director. Each still is accompanied by an effective slogan. Clearly all three stills are 'fit for purpose', that is they can be used by journalists when creating features on the new film.

6: The evaluative analysis

Evaluative analysis (10 marks)

Once you have completed your final production you must then reflect and analyse just how successful you thought it was. You should think about the decisions you made and how they affected the overall success of your product. You do not need to consider your pitch or pre-production work unless you feel it was a key factor in realising your final production, e.g. a script or storyboard which enabled you to structure a film sequence much more effectively.

The specification requires you to analyse three key areas:

● How you used technical and creative skills.

● How you used an appropriate format with appropriate codes and conventions.

● How you were able to demonstrate an understanding of film language, organisations and audiences.

Let's look at Leo's initial assessment of a film sequence he created:

Strengths	Weaknesses
● Audience – met the brief's criteria by creating tension and suspense.	● Narrative plot holes (for example, there were meant to be five boys, although there were only three in the film extract and there was a French flag on my jacket but I was meant to be English).
● Technical skills – editing of production matches the pace of both soundtracks used.	● Technical skills – continuity errors (such as lying down in terrorist container then in the next shot sitting up and Anthony diving twice).
● Genre and audience – the audience understood the iconic war film references (i.e. *Platoon, Apocalypse Now*).	● Geographical errors (how Anthony is shot in one place then dies in clearly a different location for the sake of camerawork).
● Genre and audience – humour? ('Can I be Private Ryan?'- 'No'.)	● Technical skills – the wind spoilt some of the diegetic sound and made some dialogue difficult to hear.

You could make a chart like this of the strengths and weaknesses of your production and then expand on them in your analysis using three headings which correspond to each of the specification areas – technical and creative skills, format and codes and conventions, audiences, film language and film organisations.

Moderator tip

Show your production to a test audience to receive invaluable feedback which will help form your evaluative analysis. Break your analysis down into sections and use sub-headings to help you focus on each aspect of the process.

Leo's evaluative analysis of his film sequence

My storyboard really helped me visualise 'War Game'. I was conscious not to create a sequence that was shot from just eye level as I wanted to create fast-paced action scenes and visual variety for the audience. It also gave me a clear vision of what I wanted to shoot and so this was time-saving for me on the day of the shoot. Through my storyboard I learnt to appreciate cinematography. I found that lots of different shots of the same subject are necessary to give more choice in the editing process. It helped me understand how to create different perspectives, for example, a shot that I thought was really effective was a POV shot from both the protagonist's and antagonist's POV.

I used a shot/reverse/shot sequence so the audience could be more integrated with the action.

Shot-reverse shots draw the audience into the action

I think I met the brief's criteria by creating tension and suspense in my film extract. I have achieved this in a number of ways. Firstly, the editing of my production matches the pace of both soundtracks I used. The first soundtrack (The End by The Doors) is effective is setting a tense and melancholy atmosphere whereas the second soundtrack (In The House In A Heartbeat by John Murphy) is effective in helping create a fast-paced tense scene as the music is also quite fast paced and runs parallel to the action. Both of these pieces work excellently with the extract I believe and I am very pleased about how well they worked.

I am also pleased with the homages I made to classic war films. In the film 'Rambo', Sylvester Stallone prepares for combat in a series of quick cut edits that have become iconic. I interspersed my footage with references to this scene; for example, I daub my face with mud and speed this up to look feral.

Close-up: Daubing my face – a reference to *Rambo*

Another shot that I am proud of is my homage to 'Platoon'. This is an iconic gesture to convey the futility of war and I mirror it in 'War Game' (although the audience will hopefully laugh at this as all I'm doing is role playing with friends in the woods). I even wore my 'Platoon' T-shirt but you can't really see the image.

Platoon and War Game: Spot the difference!

I think the representation of characters in 'War Game' is really obvious. I liked the faceless terrorist backlit to create a sinister silhouette. I tried to anchor the text by placing an Iraqi flag and an Arabic political poster on the door of the hostage holding cell but am not sure if this makes the setting clear.

The representation of the boys is also clear – they are a group of friends who enjoy re-enacting war films. They are innocent and don't understand what war is really like and see it as just a game (hence my film's title). I like the element of humour as they leave the woods and Antony asks 'Tomorrow, can I be Private Ryan?' and Will and I curtly reply 'No'. I think the humour lifts the previous tension but also makes it sad as we see the young boys walk away to their fate.

I showed a draft of my production to a test audience who commented that they were not sure about how the two separate locations (the lock up and the woods) were linked and when I explained that the film begins with the end of the plot (a cyclical narrative), they didn't realise this. So I had to think of a way to make the sequencing of the narrative clearer. I decided to use a text break to anchor the time gap 'Six months earlier…' to take the action back in time and I think this is now more effective in terms of story-telling.

Overall, I am very pleased with my work and feel I have learnt a lot about the industry.

Moderator feedback

Leo demonstrates a strong creative engagement with every element of his coursework. His practical work is consistently interrogated in terms of how meaning and response is created. Written communication is excellent and terminology is confident.
The specification says you can present your evaluative analysis in any of the following forms:

- A discursive essay
- A digital presentation with slide notes (such as PowerPoint)
- A suitably edited blog.

Leo has chosen to present his analysis in essay form and has made excellent use of stills from his production to illustrate key points. He manages to cover all three of the specified areas for analysis in an engaging, thoughtful way. He interrogates his work rigorously, explains his working processes clearly and incorporates a strong personal response. This isn't simply a description of 'what I did' but a thoughtful evaluation of what his production revealed about the three key study areas. However, he has exceeded the 500-word limit. This could have been avoided by using subheadings covering the three specified areas and then just selecting key moments which clearly demonstrate his practical, technical and creative understanding of each area.

Glossary

Aerial shot: A variation of a crane shot, usually taken from a helicopter. This is often used at the beginning of a film, in order to establish setting and movement.

Alter-ego: A person's second or alternate personality.

Ambient sound: The sounds of a given location or space, e.g. a wood with leaves rustling, birds singing, waterfall splashing.

Analyse: To consider, review and evaluate.

Archetype: An instantly recognisable representation of a character that has been in use for a very long time.

Autocracy: A dictatorship or absolute rule by one person.

Back lighting: Adds a sense of depth to shots. In film, the background light is usually of lower intensity. More than one light could be used to light uniformly a background or alternatively to highlight points of interest.

Back story: The history of a character that has happened prior to the events in the film's narrative.

Beliefs: Something that you accept as true.

Benign: Kindly, friendly.

Binary opposites: Characters or ideas that represent sets of opposite values, e.g. good and evil, light and dark.

Bird's-eye view: A camera shot that shows a scene from directly overhead, a very unnatural and strange angle.

Blockbuster: A big budget film that takes over $100 million at the US box office.

Budget: The amount of money spent on either making the movie or marketing the movie or both.

Buzz: The amount of collective activity, chatter or 'noise' surrounding the release of a movie.

Canon: The accepted or official history of character(s).

Cause and effect: Cause is the specific action a person does which leads to effect or consequence of the action, undertaken by the person.

Central image: A large image on, for example, a magazine or poster, designed to stand out. Often features one star who looks straight out at the audience.

Character heading: The name of the character in a film script who is about to speak (usually capitalised and centred above the dialogue).

Chronologically: A sequence of events arranged in order of occurrence.

Cinematography: This refers to the use of framing, the movement of the camera and can cover areas like the use of lighting and colour as well.

Close-up: A shot that is close up to its subject, e.g. the head and shoulders of a subject showing facial expressions.

Colour palette: The assortment or range of colours used by the film-maker.

Comic books: American comic books that are usually monthly titles that are aimed at teenagers.

Conformity: An action or behaviour that fits in with the established way of doing things.

Connotation: Refers to the meaning we may associate with what we see on the screen.

Continuity editing: Editing that is 'invisible' producing a seamless, clear narrative.

Contradict: To deny, or argue the opposite of something.

Convention: The 'rules' of the genre – micro and macro aspects the audience expect when considering a named genre.

Cover lines: The main cover line in a magazine. It is often situated directly below the masthead. Other cover lines, often called 'puffs', are typically placed at the sides of the cover. They tell us what articles are in the magazine.

Cross-cutting: Editing that alternates shots of two or more lines of action occurring in different places, usually simultaneously.

Culture: The customs, standards and beliefs of a particular community or civilisation.

Cyclical narrative: A story that begins at the end using one or a series of flashbacks to construct the whole narrative, finally returning to where it began in time and space.

Decode: To convert a coded message in order to examine its meaning.

Denotation: This refers to what we see on the screen.

Depth of field: The term used to describe the area in focus within the frame.

Dialogue: What the characters say in a film.

Diegesis: The fictional film world as described in the story.

Diegetic sound: Sound that is part of the film's world, e.g. dialogue, a dog barking or the wind blowing.

Discrimination: Unjustifiable treatment given to different people or groups.

Dissidence: Disagreement with the established government.

Dissolve: A transition which involves one image being slowly brought in beneath another one.

Dissonant: Unpleasant use of sound or notes. A lack of harmony.

Distribution: Deciding where a film will be shown and publicising this.

Dolly/tracking shot: The camera is placed on a moving vehicle and moves alongside the action, generally following a moving figure or object.

Duality: Denoting two opposing forces within a particular character's personality, e.g. good and evil.

Elliptical editing: Shot transitions which omit parts of the story that are not significant, leaving the audience to 'fill in the gaps' in time and/or space.

Enigma codes: Narrative questions/puzzles aimed at maintaining audience interest.

Ensemble led: When a group of big stars are used as the USP (unique selling point) for a film.

Episodic narrative: A story divided into separate episodes usually based around different characters.

Ethnicity: How people are identified in terms of their ancestry.

Exhibition: Where the film is shown – cinemas of varying types.

Extreme long shot /establishing shot: This is a shot, usually from a distance, that shows us where we are. Often used at the beginning of a film to suggest where the story takes place. When the extreme long shot is used in this way it is called an establishing shot.

Eye-level shot: This shot involves positioning the camera as though it is a human actually observing a scene, usually around 5–6 feet off the ground.

Fade: A fade signals a movement in time and/or space in a sequence. There are usually two types of fade – a fade to white, or a fade to black. Both feature a smooth, gradual transition from a normal image to either a completely white or black screen

Fans: The audience that has a greater level of involvement or interest in a film than the average spectator.

Filler lights: These are used to achieve levels of brightness and eliminate shadows.

Flashback: A narrative device in which the action is interrupted by scenes representing a character's memory of events experienced before the time of the action.

Flashforward: A narrative device where future events (or events imagined by a character) are shown.

Foreground: The front of the frame.

Foreshadow: To give an advance sign of something that may happen.

Formulaic: Where a film contains the same ingredients as others.

Frame: The edges of the picture, and what is contained within the space they surround.

Franchise: Where a film and its often planned sequels are part of a larger business entity.

Function: The special purpose or task.

Gender: What is expected of a man or woman in a particular society or culture.

Generic types: A certain personality, or type of character seen repeatedly in a particular genre.

Genre codes and conventions: The list of 'ingredients' you would expect to see in a film belonging to a named genre.

Globalised: Worldwide, universal, wide-ranging.

Gothic horror: Atmospheric horror based on supernatural creatures such as ghosts coming back from the dead to seek revenge.

Graphic match: The creation of a strong visual similarity between shots, encouraging the audience to make connections between two shots.

Hand-held: Hand-held cameras often denote a certain kind of gritty realism. They can make the audience feel as though they are part of a scene.

High angle shot: The camera is elevated above the action using a crane to give a general overview. High angles make the object photographed seem smaller, and less significant.

High key lighting: The use of several lights in order to create a bright, clear environment.

Hook: The method used to attract an audience.

House style: Particular colour, font style, layout and design used in print media which help an audience to identify a product.

Iconography: The recurring symbols that carry meaning from film to film.

Ideology: A system of values, beliefs or ideas that are common to a specific group of people. All movies will have these, often whether they like it or not.

Identify: To pinpoint or see clearly.

Iris edit: A technique used to show an image in only one small round area of the screen.

Jeopardy: Danger or harm and the feelings of fear and anxiety it creates.

Jump cut: A fast transition designed to bring something to the audience's attention suddenly.

Key light: The main light used in a lighting plan.

Linear narrative: A story that is told chronologically. Films with a linear structure typically organise stories into a cause and effect pattern where the consequences of one action lead on to something else.

Long shot: This can contain a complete view of the characters, so viewers can see their costumes and perhaps recognise the relationships between them. Long shots often give us background to look at as well as the action.

Low angle shot: The camera is placed below the action increasing the feeling of height in terms of characters and structures.

Low key lighting: This uses fewer filler lights in order to create distinctive areas of light and shadow.

McGuffin: An object the securing of which sometimes drives the narrative forward.

Macro elements: The overview, the big picture, the themes and issues.

Mainstream cinemas: Cinemas (typically multiplex) that are often part of a cinema chain and predominantly feature big budget American productions.

Masthead: This contains the name of a magazine. Typically it is placed near the top of the page and is big and bold so it stands out from its competitors.

Medium or mid shot: Typically contains a figure from the knees/waist up and is normally used for dialogue scenes, or to show some detail of action.

Metropolis: A large city, usually the capital city of a nation.

Mise-en-scène: Literally what is 'put in the frame'.

Mode of address: The tone, or written style of a magazine article. How it talks to or appeals to its audience.

Montage: A film editing technique in which a series of short shots are edited into a sequence to condense space, time and information.

Mood: A particular kind of atmosphere.

Moral: A sense of right or wrong.

Motif : A repeated idea or symbol.

Motivation: The cause of an action of some kind.

Multi-platform: Properties that appear in more than one format, e.g. comics, films, TV, games.

Negotiated reading: Where a spectator agrees with some but not all messages and values in a film.

Non-conformity: Actions or behaviours which go against the 'normal' or established way of doing things.

Oblique/canted angle: The camera is tilted (not placed horizontal to floor level), to suggest imbalance, transition and instability.

Omniscient: Knowing everything, God-like.

Omniscient narrative: A narrative which allows us to know more about the characters and their situations than they know themselves.

One-dimensional character: An undeveloped, minor character only briefly shown.

Oppositional reading: Where a spectator disagrees with or dislikes the film's messages and values.

Origin story: A narrative that explains how a character came by their powers and became a Superhero.

Original screenplay: A script for a film based on a 'new' idea and not an existing property.

Pace: The speed and rate of sounds, series of shots and movements within the shots.

Pan: Camera movement along a horizontal axis.

Panel: A single frame or picture in a comic book.

Parallel narratives: When two or more characters share different stories that centre on the same event.

Political imperative: Demanding a political solution to an urgent problem.

Preferred reading: When a spectator understands and largely agrees with the messages or values evident in a film.

Production: Activities involved in the actual making of the film.

Property: Any source of ideas that has been used to create a film.

Realism: A believable representation of people, places and events.

Re-boot: When or a comic or franchise is started again almost from scratch without reference to the previous version(s).

Recurring features: Features that are repeated throughout a film.

Redemption: Improved or saved.

Restricted narrative: A narrative where the audience only knows as much as the characters know.

Revenue or box office: The money a film generates in ticket sales. A reference to where people traditionally buy their tickets.

Rhythm: The regularity of sounds, series of shots and movements within the shots.

Scene: Screenplays are divided into scenes. Each scene covers dramatic action taking place at a particular place at a specific time.

Scene direction: This refers to the action, what the audience will see when they are watching the film.

Setting: The place, time and scenery of a story.

Shallow focus: A function of a narrow depth of field and it implies that only one plane of the frame will remain sharp and clear (usually the foreground).

Slug line: The scene heading which indicates whether the action takes place inside or outside, where it is and what part of the day it is.

Social class: A group of people who have similar levels of wealth, status and influence.

Social realism: A style of film-making which deals with social issues and uses specific stylistic techniques.

Sound bridge: Sound which carries over from one scene to another often forcing the viewer to make connections between the scenes.

Soundscape: A sound or combination of sounds that forms or arises from a particular kind of environment.

Spectacle: Refers to an event that is memorable for the appearance it creates.

Sphere of action: The part of a film or story in which a particular action or activity occurs.

Split-screen: When a film is edited with more than one sequence happening simultaneously on screen.

Star ratings: Usually 5 stars indicating how highly a film has been critically rated.

Stereotype: A widely used but oversimplified image of a particular type of person. A quick way of categorising groups of people

Stock characters: Simple, fairly one-dimensional characters who invariably act according to audience expectations

Straight cut: A smooth transition from one shot to another.

Strapline: Situated at the top of a magazine page just above the masthead, designed to make the reader want to open the magazine and read on.

Studios: Organisations that arrange funding to make and distribute films.

Stylised: Having a distinctive or elaborate look.

Tagline: A memorable phrase that sums up a film, e.g. *Jaws* 'Just when you thought it was safe to go back in the water'.

Tent pole film: A film, the success of which, will 'hold up' or support the studio's other projects.

Terminology: The words or phrases uses in a particular subject.

Three-dimensional character: A film character that shows all the complexity of a real person, e.g. not entirely good or bad.

Tilt: The camera is fixed and tilts upwards or downwards.

Top lighting: When the upper areas of a subject are lit (outlined) by a source generating from above it.

Transition: A film editing technique by which scenes or shots are combined.

Two-dimensional character: A character that features more at the forefront of the story but has no complexity or depth, e.g. purely good or bad.

Urban: The inner city both its population and businesses.

Values: Moral principles or standards.

Value system: The principles of right and wrong that are accepted by an individual or a social group.

Vicariously: To experience something indirectly or via a substitute.

Viral marketing: Items that spread like a virus from fan to fan or media outlet to media outlet. They are passed from one to the other motivated by interest and curiosity.

Voice-over/narrator: The telling of a story and the information supplied to the audience by a voice coming from off screen who may or may not be a character in the story.

Vox pop: Comes from the Latin phrase *vox populi*, meaning 'voice of the people'. It most commonly refers to the kind of random interview conducted in the street.

Wipe: A transition between shots in which a line passes across the screen, eliminating or 'wiping out' the first shot as it goes and replacing it with the next one.

Zoom: Moving the camera lens in or out to bring us either closer to or further away from the action.

Index

Image credits